Bubbe Meisehs
by
Shayneh Maidelehs

an anthology of poetry by

Jewish Granddaughters
about
Our Grandmothers

edited by

Lesléa Newman

Printed in the United States of America by McNaughton & Gunn. ISBN: 0-939821-00-1

"Elegy" © by Andrea Hollander Budy was published previously in *Plainsong*. "My Grandmother, The Revolutionary" © by Sandra Gardner was published previously in *The Mainstreeter Magazine* and *Footprint Magazine*. "Advice From Nana" © by Judyth Hill was previously published in *The Baker's Baedeker*, a collection of Judyth Hill's poems. "Grandmother" © by Ruth Harriet Jacobs was part of *Button, Button, Who Has the Button?* a poetic drama about women's lives (Crones Own Press, 310 Driver Street, Durham, North Carolina, 27703). "*Rozhinkes Mit Mandlen*" © by Irene Javors is included in *Sarah's Daughters Sing* (K'Tav Press, 1989) "The Lost Pearl" © by Susan Kan is the introductory poem in *Signs of Life: The Letters of Hilde Verdoner-Sluizer from Westerbork Nazi Transit Camp, 1942-44*; eds: Francisca Verdoner-Kan and Yoka Verdoner (Acropolis, Inc., 1989). "I Was Four . . ." © by Lyn Lifshin appeared in *Raw Opals* (Illuminated Press). "The Healer" © by Rochelle Shapiro Natt was previously published in *Pearl*-Fall 1989-Volume 9. "Legacy" © Lesléa Newman first appeared in *Love Me Like You Mean It* (HerBooks, 1987). "1932" © by Lynn Saul is included in *Sarah's Daughters Sing*, (K'Tav Press, 1989). "Grandmother Sophie" © by Susan Shapiro was first published in *Present Tense*. "Grandmother's Story" © by Enid Shomer appeared in *California Quarterly* © 1985, and in *Stalking the Florida Panther* (Washington, D.C.: The Word Works, 1987) and is reprinted with the permission of the author. "Braiding My Daughter's Hair" © by Marcy Sheiner was previously published in *A Shout in The Street*, Volume 3. No. 1, *The Witness*, and *Poetry SF*. "For The New Year" © by Joan Seliger Sidney was previously published in *Midstream, Anthology of Magazine Verse and Yearbook of American Poetry, 1986-1988* edition, and *Deep Between The Rocks*, a chapbook of Joan Seliger Sidney's poetry (Andrew Mountain Press, 1985). "Sarah In Her Daughter's House With Fancy Faucets Remembers the *Shul*" © by Susan Fantl Spivack was previously published in *Greenfield Review*, Volume #12, # 1 and 2, Summer/Fall 1984, p. 136. "Sharing the Wisdom" © by Elaine Starkman was previously published in *Beyond This Body* (Sheer Press, P.O. Box 4071, Walnut Creek, CA 94596). "Family Picnic" © by Judith Steinbergh was previously published in her book, *Motherwriter* (Wampeter Press, 1983). "Traub, In My Grandma's Words" and "Leaving Traub, My Grandma's Story" © by Judith Steinbergh were published in the magazine *Newstories*. "Little Jenny" © by Barbara Unger was previously published in *Inside the Wind* (Linwood Publishers, 1986)."Immigrant" © by Linda Watskin was previously published in the chapbook, *A Measure of Gifts*, (Rising Tide Press). "It's Indian Summer" © by Anne Whitehouse was previously published in *The Surveyor's Hand*, 1981.

Contents

Dedication:

For My Grandmother, Ruth Levin

Two gnarled tree trunks from Russia
are Grandma Ruthie's hands,
gold wedding band forever trapped
under one swollen knuckle.
Her kitchen is the closest I've come
to the Promised Land.
She cooks perfect Jewish delicacies
until "they're done"
and frowns as my *matzo* balls sink
to the bottom of vegetarian chicken soup
that never makes anybody all better.

Everytime I kiss
her old apple-doll face good-bye
she hands me five dollars to buy "something nice"
though her bagels go butterless that week.
She asks if I know how to make her happy
before she dies (Don't talk silly, Grandma,
you'll live forever)
But the evidence is there:
the winter postcards from Florida
arrive in someone else's printing
and she calls me Scott in the morning
when I bring up her tea.
Yes Grandma, I know how to make you happy,
but I'll never give you a great-grandchild
only a love poem I hope you understand.

> —Lesléa Newman
> (First poem ever
> written, at age 20)

Introduction

The idea for this anthology came to me as I was speeding down 95 South, en route from Northampton, Massachusetts, to Brooklyn, New York, to visit my 98 year old grandmother, Ruth Levin, who had just moved into a nursing home. I had Yiddish music on the tape deck and tears were streaming from my eyes as the realization hit me—my grandmother was not going to live forever. I knew she was old, but she had always been old, ever since I was born, 33 years ago, and named for her husband, my Grandpa Louis, who died three months before I was born. No matter what I was going through, from the terrible twos to the throes of adolescence, from my post-college identity crises to my oh-my-god-I'm-thirty hysteria, the one thing I could count on was a pair of open arms and a bowl of chicken soup in that tiny rent-controlled apartment in Brighton Beach, where my grandmother had lived since 1940. Now she was in a nursing home and I faced the prospect of losing not only my grandmother, but precious stories that told of a whole way of life, for, to my knowledge, she was my last living relative who was born in the old country.

My grandmother and I have always had a special relationship; I am her only daughter's only daughter. Even when no one else in my family would speak to me, my grandmother would call. "I don't stand on ceremony," she would say. "Come, I'll make you *blintzes*." "With applesauce?" I'd ask. "Applesauce, sour cream, whatever you want. For you I would do anything." And she would. Nothing was too good for her granddaughter, her *shayneh maideleh*. "And not only is she pretty," my grandmother would *kvell*, "but so smart she is too, a writer she is, everything I say she puts in a book."

I would tease my grandmother about writing the story of her life, The Book of Ruth. At first she would try to discourage me. "What can I tell you? I'm an old lady, it's not so important, I had an ordinary life." But as she grew older, her attitude changed: "So many questions she's always asking me, my granddaughter: *Bubbe*, what did you do here, *Bubbe*, what did you do there, *Bubbe*, what did you eat, where did you sleep, what did you wear? Alright, if you're gonna put it in a book, listen carefully, I want you should get it right."

And so I listened. I listened very carefully because my grandmother never let me tape her, though I begged and pleaded with her. She wouldn't say why, but I think she wanted to make sure I really heard her, heard her with my bones and my blood and my heart. I spent a lot of time with her at the nursing home. Other members of my family would visit, but she didn't tell them the same stories. "You I can talk to," she would say. "You

1

understand." We have the closeness of a mother and daughter, yet since there is a generation between us, we have enough distance to accept each other, love each other, and even admire each other. Sure, we disagree plenty, and each of us is always right, but we live with our differences and forgive each other quite easily.

I met many old Jewish women in my grandmother's nursing home and I felt sad that I couldn't write down all their stories. That's when I decided to put out a call for *Bubbe Meisehs by Shayneh Maidelehs*. *Bubbe Meisehs*, literally, Grandmother Stories, is the Yiddish equivalent for old wives' tales. *Shayneh Maideleh*, usually exclaimed by a Jewish grandmother pinching her granddaughter's cheeks, means beautiful girl.

As manuscripts began arriving in the mail, my suspicions were confirmed—each woman who sent her writing told me how special her grandmother was to her, how much it would mean to have her story in a book. Even if grandmother and granddaughter didn't get along, even if they didn't particularly like each other, it was clear that a very unique bond had been formed and that each grandmother had profoundly affected her granddaughter's life.

I read over 300 manuscripts, and I was sorry I couldn't use them all. They came from as close as three blocks away, and as far as Israel, Australia, and the Virgin Islands. They came from high school women, grandmothers, lesbians, orthodox women, atheists, professional writers, and women who had never written a poem before in their lives. I was overwhelmed with short stories and poems, and as the book evolved, I decided to make it a collection of poetry. Besides making the project somewhat manageable, the shortness of the poems made the book feel almost like an old photograph album, with snapshots of each woman's life. And it was the poetry I received in the mail that made me laugh and cry and call a friend to say, "Listen to this one!"

Many of the manuscripts contained Yiddish words and phrases. They appear in this anthology in italics. (Hebrew words also appear in italics.) The variety of spellings of Yiddish words indicates different pronunciations according to where one is from. (The only "correct" way to spell a Yiddish word is by using Hebrew letters.) I chose not to standardize the Yiddish spelling in order to reflect these differences and to show what happens to language when a people is dispersed. A Yiddish glossary appears at the end of the book, for readers not familiar with these words.

Make yourself a nice bowl of chicken soup and read these poems. Read them aloud to your grandmother or your granddaughter, to your mother, your lover, your friend. Read them on *Chanukah* after you light the candles, or at *Pesach* as part of the *Seder*, or on a Friday night after the *Shabbos* meal.

2

Each poem is a gift, a piece of a woman's life that will not be forgotten because someone, a granddaughter, took the time to write it down. I am proud to be the editor of this book, and I humbly offer *Bubbe Meisehs by Shayneh Maidelehs* to Jewish grandmothers everywhere, with love and respect for your courage and your dignity, your *tsouris* and your *naches*, your humor and your bitterness, and most of all, for your stubborn insistence upon survival.

—*Lesléa Newman*
June 1989

Karen Sexton-Stein

Grandmother

We planted seeds
behind her house, beneath the sun
I dug with a rusty spoon and
Grandmother counted precisely
dropping the seeds of summer's corn
and pole beans
into my carefully carved spaces.

I loved kneeling so close to her—
our heads bent over the earth,
the supple brim of her sunbonnet
touching my hair like a whisper
as we moved down each brown row—
I, her shadow
and she, my world.

Pamela Gray

Letters to Meema

i.

There is a kitchen
where you are always
drinking milky coffee
from a bone-white
buffalo china mug

or standing at the stove
still in your coat and hat
browning onions, chopping
chicken livers
into a wooden bowl

There is a kitchen
where you model
your latest bargain:
a floral print dress
from Klein's or Mays'
$5.00 $2.50
"There was a little rip . . .
I made it a little bigger . . ."

There is a kitchen
where you reach
into your blue plastic tote bag
and pull out your newest
gadgets: a clam opener
egg slicer indoor clothesline

There is a kitchen
where you show me
all the xerox copies
you've made
of my report cards
and letters

There is a kitchen
where you say
"*shayneh maideleh*
sit on my lap"
and you bounce me

5

up and down, kiss
one cheek, then
say, "now the other"

ii.

We buried you
in one of your
bargain dresses

I buried
my laughter my open
heart my trust

I divide my life
into "Meema is"
and "Meema was"

It's almost even

You would say
the glass is
half full
not half empty

You would say
if life hands you
a lemon
make lemonade

You would say
"Two men looked
out of prison bars
One saw mud
the other stars"

iii.

When you slept
in my bedroom
on the rickety cot
under the window

after singing bits
of nonsense songs
in a cracked voice

and drifting slowly
into a steady snore

I used to be afraid
someone would come
through the window
in the middle of the night

and snatch you

iv.

We called it
"playing hands"

You'd lie in your cot
and reach around the side
of my headboard

I'd reach back
trying to grab
your fingers
before you grabbed mine

and we'd giggle
in the darkness

We called it
"playing tent"

A wool blanket
draped over
the kitchen table

The two of us
sitting underneath
on the linoleum floor
pretending we were
hiding together, bears
in a cave

and we'd giggle
in the darkness

V.

Dear Meema,

I finally found someone
who loves me
the way you did

someone I can love
with the same open heart
I had before you left

Sometimes at night
I pull away from her, scared
of whatever it is
that snatches people
away, and I curl
into my fear
like thick mud

Sometimes I let her
hold me so tightly
and curl into her
warm, welcoming body
feel her heart
beating against my back
our fingers entwined

and I breathe with her
in rhythm
knowing the stars
and you
are out there

Susan Fantl Spivack

Sarah in Her Daughter's House with Fancy Faucets Remembers the *Shul*

I'm remembering:
in the Old Country, you know, in the *shul*,
the men were downstairs
we women were up; we had our own cantor.
He read the prayers from a barrel
so we shouldn't see him
he shouldn't see us.
We stood round the barrel and prayed.
One Sabbath we were praying
and swaying
the cantor was chanting:
"Ladies, ladies,
you're shaking the barrelllll; please stop
shaking the barrelllll!"
We were praying and weeping!
That was our way.

We heard him, "Ladies, ladies."
maybe he was afraid
he would have to stay there
in the dark.
Maybe he thought we wouldn't let him out.
But he didn't stop singing.
We felt him move in the barrel, bump
our bodies. We leaned away,
stopped,
clapped our hands to our aprons.
Then we were laughing,
laughing so hard,
the tears came running some more.

Lesléa Newman

Poem for My Grandmother's Grandmother

I.

Minukha, Minukha, here comes your Faigl's Rukhl
running across the bridge from Russia
to Poland into your open arms.
Bubbe, ikh vil a fingerl, a shayn fingerl
your Faigl's Rukhl would say, as she squirmed
in your lap reaching for the rings
the pretty rings you sold in the marketplace
gold-filled rings set with bits of colored glass.
Nayn Mamela, du kenst nit hobn a fingerl,
you would say, for those rings became eggs and cheese
milk and *challah*, a woolen blanket for your lap
a roof over your shaved and *sheytled* head.
But one day Minukha, when your Rukhl
your Faigl's Rukhele came flying
over the bridge on her fat little legs
you held her tightly on your lap and you said
Nem Mamela   nem a fingerl   nem a shayn fingerl
nem dos shaynste fingerl in der gantser velt.
Rukhl clapped her hands and picked out a ring
a pretty ring   a gold-filled ring set with bits of red glass
red glass that shone in the sun
like the flames of Faigl's candles
on her beloved *Shabbos*
red glass that shone
like the flames that were to burn up the bridge
to your little Polish town
red glass that shone
like the flames that were to burn up
your beloved *shvester* Chaya and your beloved *shvester* Golda
under the Nazis' hands in the years to come
Oy Minukha how the tears fell from your eyes that day
as though you knew what was to be
when you placed the ring   the pretty ring
the gold-filled ring set with bits of colored glass
into Rukhl's tiny hand before you sent her back
over the bridge from Poland to Russia
to America, standing on a big ship
with one *klayn henteleh* holding tight to her *Mame*
her other hand holding the ring
the pretty ring   the ring from her *Bubbe*

the gold-filled ring set with bits of red glass
dos fingerl   dos shayn fingerl
dos shaynste fingerl in der gantser velt.

II.

Minukha, Minukha, I never knew your name
until yesterday   yesterday when I sat with your Rukhl
your Faigl's Rukhl   and I said to her
Bubbe, ikh vil a meiseh   ikh vil a Bubbe Meiseh
Bubbe, du gedenkst deyn Bubbe?
And my grandma Ruthie, your granddaughter Rukhl
shut her eyes as her mind flew across the bridge
from Brooklyn to Russia to Poland
to visit a little town that no longer exists.
Meyn bubbe, ikh gedenk nit meyn bubbe, she said,
no, *Mamela,* my grandmother I don't remember.
She opened her eyes to see my eyes,
dark brown like her own, filling with tears.
Then she took my hand, Minukha,
and she said wait, wait a minute
rings, rings she sold in the marketplace
rings like you got on your finger
gold-filled rings set with bits of colored glass.
My *shvester* Tzivia named her oldest for my *bubbe,*
Minnie, Minnie her name was.
Say it in Jewish, Grandma.
In Jewish? In Jewish it would be Minukha
now you know your great-great grandmother's name,
alright already enough with the crying
oy Mamela, such a *shayneh maideleh* you are
but always the tears are falling from your eyes.
Come, we'll go down for supper.
And so Minukha, down to eat we went
and then I kissed my grandma Ruthie
your granddaughter Rukhl
and left her nursing home with a gift
a gift more precious than a ring
even a gold-filled ring set with bits of red glass
lost long ago
a gift of a name no longer forgotten
a name to whisper into the darkness
when I am alone and afraid
a name to chant on the *Shabbos*
or sing aloud on the Holy days
a name to turn to in times of trouble

11

Oy Minukha, what would you have done?
a name to wrap around my heart
like a string around my finger
or a ring or a *fingerl* so I shouldn't forget
a name to shout to the world
a name to sing like a lullaby
a name that means to rest
Minukha   Minukha   Minukha

Linda Shear

One Solid Piece

In the corner of the kitchen
where the counter meets the slanted roof
tucked behind the toaster, stands
on its end, my grandmother's rolling pin.
A pin cut from one solid piece of wood
by hands turning and smoothing it
to make it ready to take hands
that would turn and use it to smooth.

Smooth—one of those words
that sounds like what it is. My grandmother
had never even heard the word
when she climbed up to the ship
that would carry her to America.
She brought so little with her—
"Bring only what you can carry Basha
only what you can manage by yourself."

Carrying her bags, Basha moved around
that tiny house in the Warsaw *shtetl*
and glanced her goodbyes.
Her eyes caught the smoothness
of one solid piece of wood
and she snatched it from the corner of her kitchen
where the table met the slanted roof.
Turning it in her hands
she smelled the warmth of her mother's kitchen
the endless loaves of bread and *pletzles*
and she knew she must make room
to carry this solid piece to America.
Turning it in her hands
she knew she would have to make room
for this legacy.

Judith Steinbergh

Family Picnic

All yellow and pink, child
       you orbit my grandmother
              as if she were the sun.

She is so old
       she moves like a glacier, and you are
              the bell clear river that trails her.

Her creases map the century
       her tongue still touches a strange alphabet
              her heart slows down to a hibernating bear.

She tells you a story I have heard
       a thousand times and you gulp down
              the words like watermelon.

Holding her, you teeter over the grass
Holding you, she recrosses continents.

Judith Steinbergh

Traub, In My Grandma's Words

A small village,
A few huts.
Their roofs thatched
with straw
and when you cook
with wood, often
the sparks leap
into the straw
and the huts burn.
Traub.   Each night
poppies bloom, an
orange light rises
over the village.
Winter.   Summer.
The tongues of flames
jab at the icy stars.
Heat. And the heaven
glows like a pomegranate.
Shouts. Shadows,
the dark forms
of families rushing
for the well, pails
passed, a hiss.
The stew expires.
Potatoes scorch
in ash, another hut
opens like a child's mouth
to the Russian sky.

Judith Steinbergh

Leaving Traub, My Grandma's Story

I'm ready, all
I can carry packed,
a few skirts,
a blouse my sister gave me
before she left,
a cloth of lace for *Shabbas*
if we live to celebrate,
a bible streaked
and stained, and this
ring that creased
my mother's finger
until she died,
this ring, I twist
trying to ease the pain.
It is spring, *Pesach*
will arrive just as we leave.
Beneath the last patches
of snow, the new grass,
the young blades of flowers
stir. The old village
rustles under the sun,
moisture rises from under the thatch,
and the black birds cackle.
The few men left
have gone to plow.
Ruts of mud glisten
and tug at wagon wheels.
I will leave this place,
this home. The land will be
torn from me like the pages
of a book and all my life,
if I should live it,
I will read the lost words
directly from my heart.

Cynthia Sobsey

English As a Foreign Language   1927

new on the block
and shy
children stared called her odd names

at school she sat in the back
a boy dipped her long blond braid
   in black ink
a girl stuck out her tongue

at home she asked momma
what is a greenhorn
·what is a kike
momma sighed   lit the Sabbath candles
and prayed in Hebrew

the teacher called her Rachel
not Ruchel   read Walt Whitman
assigned homework
a poem

so she began line by line
pulling words from behind her teeth
over the lips
onto the paper

flooding each ear
was Polish and a hard new
sound

reading the letters   shaping the words
OH SAY CAN YOU SEE

Talmudic syllables on her tongue
songs of the *shtetl* pulsing the page
with that Nightingale from Cracow

she got an A in class
held her new words like the star spangled banner

Enid Shomer

Grandmother's Story

My grandmother *shlepped* these
candlesticks all the way
from Shepatovka, Russia.
Her face is still stuck
in the luster, her fingerprints
in the patina. At fifteen
she clutched them, her only
treasure from the *shtetl.*
No more rain rolling like dice
on the tin roof, no more
snow groaning as it slipped
from the eaves.

They were lit in steerage
for three weeks of ocean
against the lust of Italian men.
She told how at Ellis Island
the inspector eyed the heft
of solid brass in her hands.
He changed her name to Feldman
to suit the length of the line.

As though viewed through a keyhole
the house I remember shines
in their polished stems: dark parlor,
oriental rug, shadowbox
of thimbles.

Later she grew rich and learned
English.
Later she said the candlesticks
were a gift from the Czar.

Ruth Harriet Jacobs

Grandmother

My grandmother, Marmita
was given the name Minnie
at Ellis Island
and carefully traced it
on the report cards
of five children
It was all the English
she could ever write

When her oldest child,
my mother, died at thirty
she took a ten year old
and a three year old
and traced Minnie
on our report cards
and on all those forms
to get legal guardianship
and state aid to feed us

She crocheted doilies
for the social worker
begged clothes and camps
and within a slum
kept a shining house

Half crazed
by her daughter's death
and endless poverty
she cried, screamed,
had no patience
with my brother
and even threatened me
good, too good though I was

But every Spring
somewhere in that slum
she stole lilacs
to put upon my dresser
and trace her love
forever on me

Karen Neuberg

In your dough kitchen

for Etta

They say you hid in the trunk of a tree,
stuffed your mouth with your kerchief,
held your screams.
They say black-booted riders
ripped your village.
You had to walk through blood.

Earlier, they say smoke wisps smelled
of baking *challah*. The sun on the Sabbath
watered in your mouth.

You were 13, Etta, when you left.

You let us eat raw dough.
Your daughters clacked their tongues,
but it swelled our imaginations.
We braided it into bread,
cut it into zinnia blossoms.

All you ever told me
was that you left because of the *pogroms*.
You were small and rode
steerage to America for free,
brought your family over
with money earned working
in a factory with your father.

Grandma, I was younger
in your dough kitchen than you were
when you left;
and yet, I remember:
The trees in their place. Corn
higher than my head, you between
the rows.

And more:
Your hands kneading dough.
Your hands fixing my ribbons.

Couldn't you remember anything.

20

Later, in a hospital
tubes pushed beneath your skin
swelled your hands like leavened dough.
I knew you were dying.
I knew that I would never know.

Beth A. Spiegel

Jenny's Chair

Everybody else calls their mother's mom grandma.
I call mine Jenny and that's not even her real name.
Her real name is Glucka.
Jenny came all the way from Poland to America.
She was twelve, and she travelled by herself.
Her family sent her to find a friendlier home.
My mother says Jenny carried everything she owned
    in a paper sack.
That way it wouldn't look valuable.
As long as I've been born Jenny has never left our house.
Most of the time she sits in that chair by the window.
We play games.
She lets me go into her closet and try on her clothes.
Most of them, she made herself.
That is why her hands hurt sometimes.
Jenny made her living sewing.
I rub her hands, she says that "melts the pain away."
I love to make up plays.
Jenny loves the theatre, I can make her laugh.
Laughing melts the pain away too.
When we aren't playing Jenny usually stares out the window.
I wonder what she sees.
I think she makes things up, like I do.
Daddy thinks Jenny can't hear.
I know she can, because when I sing . . .
Jenny claps and hums in all the right places.
Jenny's chair is empty now.
But it still faces the window.
I sit in it sometimes, to try and see what Jenny used to stare at.
Sometimes, when I look real hard I can see Jenny.
She is walking down a street, not the street where we live
but one in that place she called her "Old Country."
She is young and everyone is calling her Glucka . . .
. . . and in her language that means happiness.

Carolyn White

My Grandma Had A Lover

My Grandma had a lover
I never knew 'til she was dead
my Grandma whom Mother said
lived before her time.
Why was that? I used to wonder.
Now I know she lived before the time
Grandmas had lovers.
I felt very proud.
My Grandma had a lover
15 years a lover/65 a wife
to Grandpa that tyrant
who couldn't walk and couldn't see
that Grandma had a lover.

And what was he like
this Cy I never saw
who died and left
my grandparents poor?
They paid the bills
and paid for thirty years
that's what happens
when you countersign a lover.

I think him very neat
a pious Jew
who gave it up in America
where piety won't do
always a little sad
and quite polite
he wore his hat and socks and garters
with Grandma in the single bed
in the day light
of Brooklyn before the war.

It was the heyday of Schraffts
Grandma and her lover on 2 stools
sipping coffee sodas
one hand on the straw
the other hand in Cy's
his hand upon her thigh.

I wish I'd been there.

I don't mean to stain Grandma's reputation
to bring a blush beneath her rouge
besides she's in her coffin
I want a past for her I love
I like the fact she held secrets
so dear she couldn't keep them
Grandma with her white white hair
and trim neat figure
who could send back the fish at Lundy's
"It's not done right, young man"
and I sixteen and blushing.
I inherited her clothes.

I hope all Grandmas had lovers.
For they each had homes
and they each had us and those
who came between, our parents,
but frankly I doubt
we were all that much
and they being special
deserve a lover saying:
            "Is there anything else
            I can bring you, darling?
            A cup of tea? Just ask,
            I'll order a trellis of
            yellow roses & 12 peacocks
            crowing in the sun"
and Grandma with her young young hand
draws back her golden hair.

Marylyn Croman

The Grandmothers

My father's mother
wore silky dresses
printed with flowers
that thrust themselves
off the fabric
to grab nostrils and eyes.

Best I loved
the black dress
with the poppies
so red
my eyes teared,
and my mouth filled with saliva
and my head ached
with steamy, crimson dreams.

Grandma painted
nails and mouth
so that her hands
and face seemed
to bud with poppies,
she was hot with poppies,
aromatic,
teeming,
lush.

Evening in Paris cologne
clung to her ears,
to her throat,
to her wrists.
I thought it was the poppies
that scented the air.

She read radical
newspapers,
dyed her hair
the color of honey,
would not break a strike line
and shaved her long, white legs.

When she was young,
a thin Jewish mother

25

with seven children
and no money,
she left a husband
both brutal and stupid.
With an infant
in either arm
and five children
behind her,
she marched to the New World
and hacked out a life.

She said, "With me,
anything is possible.
I think it,
I do it.
That's the way it is."

My mother's mother
wore neat cotton house dresses,
cotton stockings
and black lace-up shoes.
She wore no make-up
and had a face so eternal,
I knew she was as old
as God.

She smelled of coffee,
bread and cold cream
and so did her flat.
Each afternoon, after
washing the floors,
she drank a cup of coffee
and slowly ate five raisins
she had placed in a saucer.

My mother told me
that Grandma had buried
three of her babies
in the old village.
I pictured her
solemnly scooping earth
from the plot
with the old-lady hands
that *koshered* the meat.
I saw her place,
with no tears,

three tiny bodies,
wrapped in white
in the grave.
She stared a moment
and nodded
and went home to cook the dinner,
to scrub the clothes,
to scour the floor,
to prepare for the Sabbath.

She came to this country
with five children
and an angry, weak husband
deafened by the war
who became her sixth child.

She said, "If you put
the troubles of the world
in a circle,
you end by choosing your own."

Diane Garden

Always Joy and Sorrow

I. Two Rooms

I can still see Nanny bending
over Pappy, smoothing the white cover
over his legs that couldn't move
that looked like logs under snow.
It seemed so dark even though
I know there were lace curtains
and light falling on the rose
and toast upon his tray.

Then Nanny moved into
the light to our teaparty.
We sat at her round table,
with the cloth with silver tassels
that tickled my legs and ate
rugelach sprinkled with sugar
that I licked from my hands.
When she lifted her teapot,
an old tune poured out
that accompanied her story:

she first saw Pappy sitting
in a tea shop in London, looking
wistfully out the window,
his soldier's hat was tilted,
like a boat on his wavy hair,
she walked over and pretended . . .

then Pappy grumbled again,
and Nanny went to him.
I think that she knew how
to bring roses into the dark,
and to fill a room with *rugelach*
and laughter without forgetting
the presence of sorrow.

2. One-Eyed Joker

After Pappy died, Nanny followed
my mother from room to room,
and tagged along on her errands,

like a small child with her mother.

Many years later Nanny moved
into a brand new apartment
in a building just for seniors.
She was like a bride displaying
her dowry: her mahogany matching
furniture, her quilt with bells
and bows and arcs of daisies.

I can see the four of them
playing cards at her new table.
Nanny was fluttering her hand
like a fan, whispering to
the old codger next to her.
Later, she pulled me aside
and told me he was her suitor,
but he was going to marry
an old lady with more money.
Nanny was dealt a very bad hand.
She died just two years later.

3. My Sister's Wedding

I can still see the rabbi
lifting the cup of wine
chanting thanks to God:
for the grapes in a cluster,
for the silver light
flickering on the leaves,,
for giving Adam a partner,
and joy to the couple.

Then they shattered the glass
to recall sorrow still
present in the world.
I thought of Nanny just down
the street in the hospital,
all curled up like a baby
inside its mother, with no hair.
Still, she looked so beautiful
with her pale pink head
shaped like an egg.
She kept calling "Pappy."

Then the shout of joy
—*"Mazel Tov"*—
filled the room and rose
above the sorrow the way
Nanny would lift her teacup
and tell me a story.

Cassandra Sagan

Lillian, Queen of the Kells

> Now that Nana is dead
> Now that she is everywhere
> not only Brooklyn
> Now that the sky is a wedding
> where she is always dancing
> Again, now, she can be my muse

I.

My grandmother used everything—
egg cartons empty spools packs of peanuts from the plane
wrapping scraps old cards   And wouldn't let us
give her anything:
didn't need a rug   flowers die
her old robe suited her *Possible to purchase pad
of writing paper at less cost than 'fancy' card*

"I'm well informed!" she'd insisted, insulted
when I doubted Jackie Onassis would help me find a publisher
even if her son-in-law *is* Jewish.
Gullible as Red Riding Hood

and as little. This old woman
who lived half a century in a single room
who never wanted to bother anybody
who kissed the *mezzuzah* on her doorframe
each time she passed
without wondering why
who put on red lipstick to kiss the backs of birthday envelopes
This punster who told my sister to quit smoking
because she was making an ash of herself
This spinster genuinely surprised
I kept not being through with men
This singer of ditties, this corny old crone

told to me
our last time together
"I, am reincarnated Celtic Royalty."

Pert in pedal-pushers
widebrim straw hat tied beneath her slightly uplifted chin,
over her arm

31

a cheap blue vinyl ballet bag
for a purse. "Remember this?"
she asked conspiratorily
arching an invisible brow;
prancing as if off to a wedding
but we were only going for *knishes.*
"Sure Nana I remember"
Several years back
she had sent my sister and I the identical blue bag.

2.

Death
I suppose
is singular,
the death of all one's lifetimes.
And so in death again
my grandmother
is queen of the Kells.
The intricate scroll of her handwriting
was always the clue.

Lillian gathers moonlight
in Celtic Heaven
like Rapunzel she
lets the ladder down
for me to climb
She convinces old women
to whisper me tales
through the oak limbs caught
at the edge of vision
through the forms of clouds
and the hands of children.
These women will teach me to look backwards
as if with one eye.

3.

Thank God
there is a *minyan* of old Jewish men
who each day
pray Heaven into form

Here everyone praises God without their bones
aching. Here they will dance the *hora*
or not dance the hora

in this synagogue of 10,000 lights
where a slice of *challah* is sufficient
have a little roast chicken, some *kugel*, a bite of honeycake
All chewed with actual teeth.

To whatever other death she has passed

my grandmother sets out her lawn chair
in this heaven
to watch over the Atlantic

and arrange our contracts
with the ancestors
of contemporary Jewish publishers

4.

And when the night sky
is revealed by lightning
my grandmother is saying hello

5.

I dream of her
so close   I call
to make sure she is still
in Brooklyn

"Tszt . . tszt . . tszt . ." she clucks. "My mother always told me never
to pay attention to dreams."

*But Nana
the* Talmud *says
an uninterpreted dream
is like an unopened letter*

There is a pause
If the Talmud *says so* she shrugs
it must be true.

So now in her Heavens
Lillian unfolds
a chair beside the sea
to sit
and open
all of the letters

Irene Reti

A Modern Woman

for Grananyu

Margit Grünbaum Reti—
You are a modern woman.
You believe in frozen food,
boxed spongecake and
lesbians.
At first, it was hard to accept me,
you, a doctor trained in the 1920s,
taught to believe homosexuality is a sickness,
that homosexuals molest children,
shouldn't be allowed to teach.
But these myths soon crumbled under
curiosity, common sense
and your desire to be
a modern woman.

At 88 you almost leap out of bed,
can do more sit-ups than me.
The President of the Nutrition Club uses you
as an example of good looking.
You always carry a bag of M&M's in your purse.

"Yes, you are right to be an artist," you write me.
"An artist has to learn, to learn to understand
the world, and herself."
You paint vast landscapes with solar systems,
green globular planets, the Big Sur Coast,
old women with ironic smiles.
"Here, I am an exception with my modern style," you write,
"I try to go ahead, with still more expressive colors."

When they wonder at your accent,
ask, "where are you from?"
you rise to your
full five feet of dignity and say,
"Texas, of course!"

You were born in 1900
in Budapest, Hungary,
already 39 when The War began.

34

You lost your favorite brother,
and your closest Uncle.
You took a three week course in Catholicism, converted,
immigrated to Turkey.
Survived to raise a son
who didn't tell his daughter
she was Jewish.

"Grananyu, what does it mean to be Jewish?"
I ask in the small motel room we share.
"It means you convert to Christianity and
forget about it.
I don't want that you are Jewish,
except that if they count the grandmothers
it will be too late for you too.
I'm sorry about that."

But you are full of contradictions.
You take me to Israel
on a ten day TWA getaway tour.
I cry all of our first night,
desperately lonely, 8000 miles from home.
You have no patience with me.
You have lived in Hungary, Russia, Turkey, Venezuela and
the United States
always a stranger.
"Everywhere you go, in every country, people are the same.
You must speak with them, become friendly."
In the morning we peer out of our hotel window—
dawn over Jerusalem.
"This Israel," you say,
flinging back the curtain over that golden city,
"The Jewish people have done this,
worked so hard.
Enough crying."

You invite me and my Jewish lover, Bina,
to your Orange County apartment,
give us a double bed,
a private room.
You turn to her kindly, say,
"You have a nice face, a face like my own,
a Jewish face,
not like Irene.
She doesn't look Jewish."

We take you to the Jewish Museum in Los Angeles,
stand by a stunning *menorah*—
a silver tree of life,
candles, fruit, birds
nestled in lush branches.
You and Bina discuss with great excitement
a *Shabbat* in your parents' house 70 years ago.

But I stand by
with nothing to share.

Grananyu, you never called me
Shayneh Maideleh
Bubbelah
I never even knew I was Jewish until I was 17,
never knew I had a Jewish grandmother at all.

But these things you taught me—
think seriously,
always go ahead,
never stop learning,
live.

Judyth Hill

Advice From Nana

Always wear your clothes like they have only been yours.
And never pay retail unless it's divine.
Eat only what you want on your plate and leave anything.
Eat dessert and hors d'oeuvres and skip the entrees, just enjoy.
Make men buy you presents, and if you don't like their taste,
teach them what you love.
If you can't teach them what you love, leave them.
And darling, don't pick your split ends.
Look into the eyes of the person you are talking to,
and they will believe you.
If you want to stop someone from criticizing you,
let your chin quiver just a bit, eyes fill up, yes,
there, that's it.

Don't stand in the corner at a party, walk over to the books
and enjoy them, because at least that's fun
and you should never be uncomfortable at a party, God forbid,
you are so gorgeous.
Remember I love you.
Remember to call me and tell me everything.
Remember this pearl necklace is yours, and the china.
Don't sit with your legs apart,
you're sure to get the wrong boyfriends that way, I surely did.
I had to be told a hundred times too.
Did I tell you I love you?
Lord, you look like your mother at that age,
    and she was a wild one.
I had my hands full with her, at least you got her brains.
Thank God for that, she was a whiz.

Now remember, if someone asks your name
    more than three times,
Forget them! Don't tell them!
I never would and I met everyone I needed to.
When you want to know a good restaurant in a strange town,
don't ask at the hotel, just walk a bit, read the menus,
and smell the air when you walk in.
You can always tell by the smell.
And Darling, even a good man can be picked that way. . .
I always found good men by their smell.

Lynn Saul

1932

Harry Saul wraps the leather straps of *tefillin* boxes
    around his arms
Harry Saul recites his prayers next to his bedroom window
watches snow layering the branches of the sycamores outside
    his window
Harry Saul prays the way his father and his grandfather prayed
on winter mornings in Lithuania

although here Harry Saul is a merchant of Michelin tires
he lets his son wear the Michelin Man suit
lets his son parade around the streets of East Liberty
    advertising Michelin tires
like some fat rubber tire man I saw just last week
marching down Stone Avenue in Tucson Arizona

and he lets his daughter hitchhike with her girlfriend
hitchhike across the continent like any young man might
also he has taught his daughter *Torah*,
he has let her go to college

and here on a snowy January day Harry Saul is in his bedroom
    praying
and his wife has just walked downstairs to make the morning
    oatmeal and coffee
and there asleep in Harry Saul's favorite wing chair is a man
normally we might call him a burglar
he just came in off the streets for a warm place to sit
it's a January morning, there is snow on the sycamores
Harry Saul's wife is surprised, she's afraid, the man is large,
    and he happens to be black
he's asleep in his overcoat, his hands are nestled
    in its torn pockets

Harry's wife goes upstairs, she doesn't scream, she asks
    her husband what to do
Harry Saul tells his wife he is praying the way
his father and his grandfather prayed in Lithuania,
he tells her to leave him alone, so she walks downstairs
she walks past the man sleeping in her husband's wing chair

she thinks of her son, overheating in the tire suit
she thinks of her daughter, taking rides from strangers

38

in Montana
she walks to the kitchen without waking the man
she makes the man oatmeal and coffee.

Nancy Berg

Ein Leben on Dein Kopf

A Blessing On Your Head, Hand, And Foot

Grandma and Grandpa
get lost at Ellis Island.
All those long lines of people who smell like
garlic
or stale beer,
or 67 days on a boat,
or *anything* outside of a *shtetl* in Russia . . .
It must be very confusing.

Somehow,
instead of Brooklyn,
they end up in New Rochelle,
where everybody else is
Irish,
or Italian,
or Black,
where the whole place is founded by
French people,
the Huguenots,
who leave France because they want to pray to Somebody
    unpopular,
or maybe because they want to pray to Somebody popular
in an unpopular way.

So Grandpa's tune
Hanteleh . . . fooseleh
sounds French inside my head.
As if the Huguenots leave behind
something in the air
that makes anything the
Irish,
or Italians,
or Blacks,
or one Jewish family
sing
sound vaguely like "Sur La Pont D'Avignon."
But this is probably my imagination.

Grandpa opens the Queen City Delicatessen
on Main Street in New Rochelle.

He gets the Irish,
and Italians,
and Blacks,
and even a few Republicans
to develop a taste for *kreplach* soup,
and stuffed *derma*
and *kugel,*
and somehow,
(perhaps another legacy of the Huguenots),
the fattest french fries anyone has ever seen.

Grandma and Grandpa
don't leave Russia because they want to pray to Somebody
     unpopular
or even pray to Somebody popular in an unpopular way.
They are widely considered to have made a poor choice
in the way they are born.
Grandma stops praying when she is twelve,
about halfway through one of the more exciting
     midnight *pogroms.*
It isn't when they are tying various parts of Uncle Abe
to various horses,
but later,
when they get the horses to gallop in various directions.
Her faith goes away
all at once,
like a virgin's pink flower.
She waits and waits,
but it never grows back.

Still, for some reason,
she keeps *kosher* all her life
She feeds me *mandelbreit*
you would never believe was baked by an atheist,
and when she takes down the combs,
she lets me sit on her lap
and brush the longest white hair in the world.

shana punam, shana keppele, shana velt.
beautiful face, beautiful head, beautiful world

Next I sit on Grandpa's lap and we do the song.
Hanteleh . . . fooseleh . . .
He puts down the Yiddish newspaper
and points out my hands, my feet.
Outside the window,

41

old men sit on benches
with or without grey fedoras,
but mostly with.
Across the street
eleven sparrows
perch on the branch of a tree.

Grandma and Grandpa are my mother's parents.
My father imagines they have somehow hurt him,
and will not allow them in our tiny apartment.
New York is full of aunts and uncles and
grandparents and cousins
on both sides
who are not allowed in our tiny apartment.
There is no room for them anyway.

They all come to me in my sleep,
in their functional family units.
They are like "Father Knows Best" or
"The Donna Reed Show,"
only these are Mediterranean people,
so they're more visibly affectionate.
I try *both* the code words to get in the circle—
hanteleh . . . fooseleh—
but they are not interested in body parts,
and certainly not extremities.

Grandma has a stroke,
and she finishes her life
in an ecumenical nursing home.
When Grandpa dies,
my mother sits *shiva* for three days.
Her tears make the first
permanent lines beneath her eyes.

When the time for sitting on wood has past,
my mother still refuses to sit on roughly
half the chairs in the apartment.
Later, when she and my father move to California
and buy all new chairs,
she refuses to sit on most of them, too.

I take my hands, my feet,
to the Midwest,
where almost nobody has ever tasted *matzoh brei*,
and nothing sounds French except Grandpa's Yiddish song.

I keep a *mezuzeh* on my door,
but from time to time
I also light a candle to the Virgin.

My prayers bounce off the walls
in a garbled hybrid
of every language
I have ever learned
even one mispronounced word of.
Still,
once in a great while,
I can swear I see
a blessing,
a *brocha*
filter out through the window screen
and perch on the branch of a tree.

Susan (Ritter) Levinkind

A Recipe

A guggle muggle
I'm not even sure how to spell it.
If my *bubbe* was still alive
perhaps she could write it in Yiddish,
holding the fountain pen so tightly
in her bent fingers
it hardly touches the page,
making letters from right to left
like little squiggles they looked to me.
My *bubbe*, sighing and *oy veying*.
She didn't learn to write
the language of her childhood
her *mame-loshn*
until after she came to America.
In night school she wrote,
peering through her glasses,
wire rims and thick round lenses,
her eyes looked huge and watery
when she wore them.
A guggle muggle
to soothe the sore throat
of her *shayneh maydeleh*.
Here it is:
an egg, mixed up
a glass hot milk
a *bissl* butter.
Drink it slowly *mein kind*,
don't burn your throat,
so good it feels, yes?

Rochelle Shapiro Natt

The Healer

Mama tells me
how Grandmother raised her ten children
in Russia, alone,
lost four in a *pogrom*,
hid the others in the woods,
walked across Europe.

I remember
Grandma dying—
her white braid of hair
coiled high on her head,
her skin taut over high cheekbones.
Once, in her kitchen,
she rolled dough
and let me turn a glass upside-down
to make sugar cookie circles.

Mama keeps telling tales:
how Grandma would heal the neighborhood
with her remedies—
goose grease in hot milk for croup,
drops of urine for sore eyes.
I want Mama to tell me how she got the cancer.
Mama says, "A tumor grew in her womb."
It sounds like a rhyme,
as if it doesn't hurt at all.

Susan Eisenberg

Grandma's Obituary

At eighty,
she drove once a week to The Montefiore Rest Home;
left the car motor running while she rushed in—disguised
as an ingenue in a short, bright-colored dress; served lunch
to the old-ones-poor-things; leaped behind the steering wheel
and careened back to her daughter's.

At eighty-two,
her bones spongy with cancer, her jalopy junked by rust,
her doctor recommended she use a cane when she walked.
"But what would my friends say!" she gasped, and died
at the thought.

Anne Whitehouse

It's Indian Summer

It's Indian summer, more beautiful than I can remember.
And still you lie across the couch, holding your death
in your hands as if it were the glass garden
your sister left you or the prism that was your husband's.
An interior you cannot reach but look at as the light
shifts and images move across the four walls of your room.
They hold you as the mountain sheering to its valley
from your window cannot hold you. Like the past holds you.
Now, while leaves pile in drifts outside your door
with no one to rake and burn them, tell me how for years
the sparrows returned to their nest in your chimney
while you knitted afghans, determined and fireless,
and black mounds of coal turned to dust in the cellar.

Marcy Sheiner

Braiding My Daughter's Hair

This is what we waited for:
a doll of flesh and blood
to rearrange, recreate, manipulate.

Interweaving silken strands
my palms come alive with memories
performing an ancient ritual.

The head on the other end
is unaware of her story
thinks it's just a hairdo.

Rhoda, whose hair hung loose
tugs harshly at my scalp
impatient with tangles and knots.

Behind her stands the ghost of Lily
who died too young
to teach the art of braiding.

Bema looms behind the ghost
magnificent silver braids
wound round and round her head.

This is what we waited for:
my fingers fly, over and through,
over and through.

Gene Zeiger

My Grandmother's Braid

I lift her
Thin braid
Air! Feathers!
She says sad
How thin it is
How thin and lonely
While everyone
Is talking
Thin tail
Long stain
Of water
Dripping down
A stout wall
What's left
After rushing
Thin braid
How it travels
Down her back
Quiet
As a wristbone
My thin body
Drifting down
The curved back
Of huge earth
Three bands
Of hair
Folded over
Thin braid
Quiet
Sparrow's
Only seed
My sorrow
When the grown-ups
Smile

Deborah Zucker

Grandma Sarah

When I was young I would ask you to show me
the rich brown braid of your childhood hair
A European girl's braid, innocently intact
your mother had cut it off when you were 14
It slept for decades in the closets of your American homes

Seeing that braid
was like glimpsing your lost teenage face
Forever young, it was unnerving proof of your childhood
a reminder
that youth is ownerless, and already mine is gone

When you went into the old home,
as we gingerly packed your vases and afghans,
I took the braid
I took it back to the city and wrapped it in a cloth
and put it in my closet

                    * * * *

Today, years later
I take the braid out
I fill a basin with warm water
and submerge it, watching the long strands relax
for the first time in 76 years.
It's like stroking your head
or bathing a young animal
to wash that braid,
watching tiny air bubbles skittering the length of it,
catching at the tail

When I finish, I lay it on the table
and, combing it out slowly I wonder
who knew you best.
And as it dries in the silence,
    I watch its dormant Jewish waves
spring soundlessly to life.

Susan Shapiro

Grandmother Sophie

The silence tells me it's Sabbath
on Delancey Street. I'm peering
through tenement windows, searching
for a woman with high cheek bones
who undoes the thick bun that binds
her dark hair.

Though we never met I seek Sophie,
the dead woman whose face I stole,
they say, from the photograph
that scared me as a child.
My mother whispered
"The Goodman women are witches."

I hold back my hair dark as blackbread.
"Grandmother, I'm in love again."
I hear thunder on the Lower East Side,
the Goodman blood rising to my cheeks
and Sophie on the fire escape
winks a Slavic eye.

Irene Javors

Rozhinkes Mit Mandlen

Mamushka, it has been so long since we have spoken.
Remember, we sat in air cooled movie houses on
warm summer afternoons in July.
I would translate the dialogue so that you
would understand the story.
Often, you would mumble to me in Russian-Yiddish
of cossacks and *pogroms*,
and tears would well up in your eyes.
I would take hold of your hand and
say, "let's have a Good Humor,"
and off we'd go in search of popsicle sticks.
In the morning, you always read *The Forward*
and argued with the ghosts of your comrades.
I'd hear you speak, with great conviction of
how Czar Nicholas deserved everything that
happened to him.
At the table, you would sip tea out of a glass
that you held in your right hand while
simultaneously taking a bite from a small
sugar cube that sat poised between thumb
and forefinger of your left hand.
This delicate balance between glass and cube
seemed quite an accomplishment to me.
A greater mystery involved your ability to
hold such a hot glass without getting burned.
You'd laugh and say,
      "It was so cold in Russia
      that I learned to hold
      fire in my palms."
Sometimes you'd forget to speak to me in English
and, you'd talk in Russian, expecting me to answer you.
I would say, "I don't understand."
You would answer, "No you are the only one
    who does understand."
Then, you'd get a strange look in your dark eyes
and hold me close to you.
When you seemed to see things that I did not,
you would speak of distant places with exotic names,
Baku, Ararat, Rostov on the Don,
and mysterious doings in the dark of night.
You smelled of farina and old newspapers.
You had an ivory comb that you delicately ran through

your wavy, white hair.
You'd tell me secrets about Russia,
the Revolution,
and the brother who you loved so very much.
You'd curse at Stalin and warn me about tyrants
who would steal our souls if they could.
I would imitate your accent and pretend
that I was a bohemian who presided over a salon
in Brighton Beach.
Mamushka, I'm all grown up now,
I don't sing your labor songs
and I have forgotten the words to
your beloved *Internationale*.
At night, as I fall asleep, I hear you
singing a lullaby of raisins and almonds.
I imagine you sitting by the window
watching for signs of spring.
So many years have passed,
all that remains is memory and your
familiar voice that speaks to me in dreams.
We made a promise to each other.
We agreed that when the Revolution comes,
we will make certain that everyone eats strawberries
and dances in the moonlight.
In this paradise of freedom,
we will rejoice in our reunion.
Until then, I say to you,
das vedonya, tovarich.
Goodbye, dear friend.

Sandra Gardner

My Grandmother, the Revolutionary

1.

My grandmother
in the Russian revolution
was a political prisoner
she watched them kill her brother
carried subversive pamphlets
in her petticoats
the Cossacks couldn't see
the iron will underneath

Coming to America
with a price on her head
she took a lover
who was not worthy
she called her factory
a sweat shop
jumped on a table
and incited a riot

2.

An old *Bobba*
making fish balls
and wonderful soup
from no money
slipping a dollar
to her little grandchildren
"don't tell *Zaydie*,
take it, take it"

Once when I was
confined to bed
with a childhood illness
a whole wardrobe
of doll clothes appeared
painstakingly sewn
on a treadle machine
by nearly blind eyes
and arthritic hands
rich fabrics
silks, satins, velvets

3.

When I grew older
she lived with us
her daughter, my mother,
ignored her
she kept to her room
a heavy volume of Schiller
and her magnifying glass
in her lap

She tried to help with the housework
to be part of the family
she didn't sleep well at night
and had to take sleeping pills
one morning she couldn't
stand her life another minute
so she took the whole bottle
and left a note in Yiddish
that no one could read

Marilyn Kallet

Anna

Hearts starve as well as bodies,
Give us bread, but give us roses!
                —Women's Union Song

No one asked Anna for stories of Russia.
We were nouveau riche on Long Island.
She was the "New York Grandma,"
surviving in Canarsie,
hiding from Cossacks
in back of her second-hand store
with her terrified daughter Marilyn.
My mother couldn't stand the smell
of poverty. She was used to Southern
gentility, iced tea, thank-you notes,
voices soft as gloves.
"I never would have married your father
if I had met his family first."
Meaning Anna and her daughter,
Nat and Sammy, her gangster sons.
My father was the only "good one."
Anna was an embarrassment, with her
housedress and frizzy hair.
As kids, her accent put us off.
When we stopped by her apartment
once a month on Sunday
she kissed us hello on the mouth.
The other Grandma smelled like rose
water but this one
gave off boiled chicken and sweat.
I got stomach-aches when we drove
the Belt Parkway to see her
so I wouldn't have to eat
her *gefilte* fish, her chopped liver.
Once Anna took down her guitar
and played us Yiddish songs.
She complained she missed the way
the lamps shone on the streets
in her village. My father silenced her,
"Remember the *pogroms!*"

When I was twelve Anna tried to give me
a yellow coat from her store.

56

Clothing was piled up everywhere,
smelling of camphor. I felt suffocated
when she helped me into the tacky yellow sleeves.
Nothing was new with Anna.
Her store wasn't sweet like Arnold Constable's
where the *Gentile* girls shopped,
where they sprayed Chanel into the air
and canaries sang in cages
above the makeup counters.
"It's wool," Anna said.

Aunt Marilyn died of cancer at thirty-three.
Anna complained more and more,
hoarded clothes and toys in her bedroom,
blocked the doorway
with "stuff for the store:"
old newspapers, a wind-up monkey
that blew bubbles.
When my father wasn't yelling at her
he was sending her money.
One Sunday she cried loneliness
from her bed in Uncle Sammy's basement.
My father shouted into the phone,
"Do you want me to put you in a Home?
Then you better learn to live at Sammy's!"
That night Anna died in her sleep.
We never tried to imagine her fears,
or how fiercely
a mother could love her only daughter.

Jesse Kulberg

Grandma

As I grow older
more and more
I remember my
little grandmother.

Tiny, barely
five feet tall
black berry eyes and
a gamin smile
and birdlike hands that
could perform magic
with a squat and ugly
ever obedient Caliban
of a coal burning oven.

But how did she manage
on those bitter stormy days . . .
when we elbowed spots of vision
and caught a joyous glimpse
of the fragile little figure
bravely battling the elements.
Never mind Mama's scolding
We'd dash down skimming along
the perilous icy street to grab
the heavy snow-filmed oil cloth bags
she carried in each hand,
Her indulgent laughter accompanied us
as we practically carried her upstairs.

There was a quick smile for mama.
For us she busied herself with
feathery kisses which we returned.
(Oh the feel of the soft lined cheeks
I still feel them now.)
Then out of those enticing
bulging bags she began to extract
secret treasures she had gathered.
Mama shook her head slipping off
the damp sweater and shawl to dry.
There were still warm chestnuts,
turkish candy and *halvah*.
Had she bought them, made them, stolen them?

She had no money, we all knew
that, and neither did we.
Who asked? Not I or my brothers or Mama
who knew better than to ask.
She watched grandma with grudging affection
who was tossing sweets into our wide open
greedy fledgling mouths.
Mama brewed hot tea in a glass
sometimes slices of apple twirled inside
or a spoonful of rose jelly mama
had made from grandma's recipe.
Just a sip and she'd smile—good, good
mama shook her head not as good as you
oh yes oh yes better than me.

They spoke in fractured English
(to please us?) spiced with Yiddish.
I was too young for it to matter
but my brothers would giggle,
look guilty and sheepish.

Came the time for showing off
mama boasted one brother got an A
in algebra. Mine goodness said grandma
very proud. And of the youngest, all sniffles
and smiles. What from you? I learned
a new song in kindergarten.
"Did you ever see a lassie?" I sang
adenoidal, mama glancing warnings
at my brothers making faces.
But grandma listened blissfully
black eyes flashing admiration
And lo and behold a special trophy
for me. A marshmallow foxy grandpa
You don't have to share she glowed.
But I did of course. In three bites it was gone.
Mama towering above her
frowned at little grandma.
You spoil them all
you're getting too old
for pushing yourself,
you're not too well.

A toss of the head, a sharp glance.
Be careful she meant let the children

enjoy. Don't spoil it
all for them.
What's a grandmother for?

A visit too soon ended. She
must be off. Of course she loved us
best but there were others. Oh no stay
grandma we cried, cunningly cajoling
bubba don't go. Oh so many kisses for that
but she'd visit again soon
or we with her.

Not long after that she died
her tender hands full
of raisins and almonds outstretched
to a child
She went with not much fuss
but with a toss of her head as if
annoyed someone dared to stop her joy
in us. Or so it seemed. We never
wondered why so much joy
in just us. She was grandma.

She is gone almost longer
than I have lived
but I cannot, I shall never
forget her.

And how I miss her how I miss her how
I miss her.

Margo Hittleman

Rose

for R.M.G. (1892-1967)

Crazy, they called you
and locked you away.
For your own good, they said.
Too much trouble, they said.
Uncontrollable—
crying, that is
tears flowing as you sat
day after day in a faded chair
unkept, unfed,   old

Your body
rejecting indignities
absorbed for decades: a disappeared husband, lost
in the wilderness of this foreign land
(did he even say goodbye?);
the greedy touch of strangers
over
          and over
                        and over
casually taking what you were forced to offer
that your children might eat

Your mind
grieving for those left behind
as you said farewell to your home
          then your new home
                        and then yet again,
following father, then husband, across the seas
the ever-wandering jew

Your tears inconvenient   embarrassing
They wished you would pull yourself together
          be happy
          find something to occupy your time
Wished you wouldn't remind them of things
they had been powerless to prevent

61

Crazy   What they call you
when you allow yourself to notice
a lifetime's measure of pain
and no one comes to hold your hand and say
I know
        I'm sorry
                I love you.

Anne Corey

Anyuta

My grandmother   Anyuta
the woman I am named for
loved to sing   dance   recite tragic Russian poetry
she was   dark   wild
my mother tells me   *you have her eyes*
        as I study the faded sepia images

Anyuta sailed to America   to change her life
        escape *pogroms*   leave persecution, Cossack attacks
the passports showed
that the man she traveled with
was her brother: her eyes alone gave the lie to this
        he was her lover, her husband
        running away from the czar's army   forced conscription
        (Jewish lives = expendable)   certain death
using her brother's passport, he had taken her last name
and they were
very much in love   packed in steerage
with bundles and *babooshkas* on the boat coming over
they made a baby: my mother

very much in love

but as newness eroded
my grandfather   was a jealous man
        many nights   my mother
        and her younger brother
        pulled the covers over their heads
        to muffle the sound of Anyuta's shouts   her screams
as she argued with the tight-lipped man
who accused her   of being herself
I imagine her screams
strange and distant   like the sea
                roaring in a spotted shell
                held cold to the naked ear
an insistent surf   echoing
through the dark, long-gone Coney Island apartment
        a spray of foreign words   Russian   Yiddish
        mixing with the English
countering those angry questions:
        why did you   look at him?
                        dance with him?

63

sing to him?   smile at him?

Once Anyuta put her children in a cab,
> said she was running away, said *we're leaving daddy*
my mother   a child   began to cry
> tears that a lifetime later she still regrets
and my grandmother changed her mind
had the cab   drive twice around the block
and drop them all   back home

she was just the age I am now   34   when she first got sick
> a stroke   the doctors said
> her heart too weak   blood too strong
>> an effect (perhaps) of the rheumatic fever
>> she had as a child   in the old country

She was never right   after that
other strokes followed
she did not   walk right   talk right
shuffling along the boardwalk   or on the sands
> bent over
>> she spent endless days in search of a cameo
>> lost years before: a shell carved by design,
>>> not water chance
>>>> into the outline of a woman;
a trinket long ago washed out to sea
> buried   crushed
or dug up by a child as cracked adornment
for yet another crumbling castle
at the edge of the ocean.

Anyuta got worse   was bed-ridden
my mother's adolescence spent carrying bedpans
> trying to convince her mother
> that the food she brought her   was not poisoned
> that her husband/my grandfather   *that man*
> was not poisoning her

One day she tried to hang herself
> looping a piece of string over a toothbrush
> dangling it from the headboard
my grandfather called the doctors
and they said   *she's dangerous   lock her up*
so he did
he put her in a hospital
committed her to the psychiatric ward

a woman not much over 40
not criminally sick   but sick
          her heart and brain and blood
          clotting and bursting
put in a cell
and beaten   yes
          my mother saw bruises
they said   *she did it to herself*
          or   *she fell*   or
          who knows?   crazy people
                    just develop welts   spontaneously

my mother/her daughter
          high school student at Abraham Lincoln/teenager
who could she believe?
she did not know what to do
          did   nothing
one day   they called and said   *claim the body*
                    your mother is   *dead*
                              claim the body
          so she did

now half a century has passed
since Anyuta died   in a cage in Bellevue Hospital

my grandmother   Anyuta
          the woman I am named for
who loved to sing, to dance, to recite
          tragic Russian poetry
She had eyes like mine.
She was dark and wild and I sometimes hear her:

          I hear Anyuta's screams.
                    Her screams.

Barbara Unger

Little Jenny

Shards of a wine goblet
shatter under the bridal *huppa.*

His stiff suit showered
by chips of paint.
A violin solo,
something old.

Later five pale children
break beneath her.

For them
she scrubs Landau's stoop
in the Harlem brownstone
on Edgecombe Avenue,

pulls the animal caul
across her face,
remembering her village,

Chagall's world,
before the sky spit
bullets and axes.

Deborah Esther Schifter

November 19, 1942

The stench, it seemed, had been there forever. The Jews of Lublin sought life while the fires of Majdanek burned. There were memories of better times, happy times even; but to this world of misery there was no beginning. The realm of smoke, ashes, and smell of burning flesh stretched infinitely far, backwards and forwards, past and future.

As ordered, Paul and Balbina joined the crowd in the street. He hunched forward, trying to offer warmth to himself underneath his worn clothes. Her arms were wrapped in a tattered shawl.

Paul turned to gaze at Balbina and thought of the *maydelech* he had known twenty-five years earlier. Her colors had faded, but she still kept her beauty—erect and assured. Her head turned slowly as she surveyed the scene. He knew that she was thinking, scheming, planning. Even now she wouldn't stop. Even now when it was hopeless.

The scene was not new. They'd watched it before—last March—from the window of their apartment on Gromacka Street. That time their names hadn't been called. This time they were taking everybody.

Paul put his hand on Balbina's elbow. Whether to offer solace or to seek it, he did not know. Balbina moved to touch a spot over her left breast. Paul's hand was left hanging in the air. Slowly he let it drop.

Under her hand, there, over her breast, was where she kept ration cards, and papers, and a picture of Richerl. He had been a child when he left four years ago. Now he was a man. This single photograph was her only glimpse into her son's manhood.

For four years she also stored her child's latest letter there, under her dress. That way it was always handy to read to her cousins, her neighbors, her friends—anyone who would listen. This last letter was held to her breast for over a year.

Paul instinctively touched his back pocket where he kept his own picture of Richie.

Balbina turned to Paul. She looked into his face, studying it for a second before she spoke. "Paul," she squeezed his hand for emphasis. "Paul, I choose differently."

She dropped his hand, turned around, and started to walk away from the crowd. Her pace was even, her head held high. "Balbina!" Paul called in as loud a whisper as he could manage. She didn't turn around, but made a gesture with her hand. I know what I'm doing, it said.

The shot's report sliced through the crowd's din and remained lodged in Paul's brain. They had hit her in the leg. She couldn't walk anymore, so she stood still, tall, straight, waiting. Paul watched her back, his fists clenched. The second shot hit her in the chest. The explosion echoed in his head, wave after wave, as she first swayed slightly; then her knees buckled, and slowly she collapsed.

Paul pictured his wife's blood spreading over the face of their son.

The guards ordered people to start walking. The crowd parted to move around Paul as he stood, head bent, facing in the direction of Balbina's body. A neighbor stopped to put his hands on Paul's shoulders, steering him into the flow. Paul moved forward along with the rest. After the walk, along with the rest, he undressed, as ordered. Then they were told to enter the shower.

Susan Kan

The Lost Pearl

for Hilde Verdoner-Sluizer (1909-1944)

Click and caught,
framed and fit in glass,
wearing black with white lace
forever knotted around your neck;
your skin is satin smooth
not grandmotherly
as I want it to be.

Looking at me with mother-eyes,
your right eye dares me
to climb alps and swim channels.
Your other dares me to write.
I try to read your life
in eyes that watch me water
plants, sit at my desk, lie
in bed reading, sleeping, making love.
These eyes stare at me in my mirror.

In rooms spread across this country,
doubles and triples of you watch
my sisters and cousins, aunt, uncle and mother.
We hold each other, silently
confirming our life and wondering who
you might have been.
I wear a ring you weren't wearing
the day they took you away.
Its three pearls come unglued and get lost
one at a time, and over and over
like a mesmerized child
I replace them as though resetting
a pearl beside the others
keeps our lives together.

With the tattered thin letters
you wrote to arbitrary survivors,
we invent a script for you: plans
for your children, for yourself,
family secrets, recipes for cooking,
recipes for living. But your mid-sentence
stories were stolen from your broad forehead

like wedding rings off fingers,
like pendants half-hidden
at the V at your neck,
like children.

I keep looking to see
if you are afraid. I want
to set you in my mind as surely
as I set this photograph on my shelf.
Heir of the ache in my mother's eyes,
I cry for your songs, the ones
you hummed as you combed your hair
to a clip at the back of your head.

Joan (Thaler) Dobbie

Mine Was Not A *Bubbe*

but an *Oma*.
When I had fever
she sat by my bed
and told me the goose
that laid the gold,
whispered
in the good chef's ear:

"Kaiserschmalze"
The King's favorite dish
(goose-egg with sugar
beaten to a fluff).

She spoke in German.
I answered in English.
Hitler's dull knife had split
our lives clean as a razor.
Fairytales were all the history
I learned from anybody.

Years later, after *Opa* died
(& I was in college)
she spent her waking hours
shredding old letters,
burning the pulp.

"Money," she told me.
"Love is a dead word."

"Beware of the poor,
the infirm,
the ugly.
Befriend only the happy.
Trust no one.
Believe nothing."

Then she died.

Joan Seliger Sidney

For the New Year

Our rabbi tells us not to live in the past
but on *Yom Kippur* to remember.
How can I remember
the grandmother I never knew?

For the New Year, Mother
teaches my children to braid *challah.*
Side by side we weave the loaves, watch
through the oven door
how they fuse like trees at night.

We thumb black and white
photos from Poland. Grandmother
stands beside ten children.
Behind them her flower garden,
stripped: chrysanthemums and asters clipped
by townspeople to honor their prince's birth.

Grandma, you lean against the fence
rereading letters your children sent
from Argentina, America, Israel
begging you to flee. You watch the old
familiar road turn black with soldiers.

Lisa Goodman

Grandmother

I.

I imagine three men
standing on the shore
of the Volga River.
It is dusk.
The sun slices into waves,
and they are laughing,
as she floats past them,
her blood mixing with water.

Her crime was a semitic face,
and a body warm,
holding secrets they longed to understand.

You were only sixteen,
Grandmother,
when you arrived to the shores
of America,
alone,
with the scar of your mother's murder
in your breasts.
I see you in your black high heels
and threaded shawl on the dock,
peering at figures passing quickly
through thin wired glasses,
startled by this land
of steel and brass.

II.

My mother tells me,
you were always old,
Grandmother,
even as you bore three children,
making your way each day
to the market,
feeding mouths open and needing you.

Your home was always by the ocean,
watching waves.
Sometimes as night descended,

73

you could hear the water weeping endlessly.

My mother tells me,
your hands shook in the evening,
as you sat rocking,
weaving your life into threaded wool.

My mother tells me,
you bought orange curtains,
placed flowers on the table
to ease the shame
she felt for worn wooden floors,
pain strewn like clothing
throughout rooms.

III.

I remember the scent of meatballs
drifting past doors.
I ran to the kitchen,
where you stood
stirring the old steel pot
stained with grease.
"It will be good,
have a little taste,"
as the spoon glided into my mouth.

You tell me now,
"a mother is a precious thing,
Lizanka.
You need her when you are
very young
and very old."

Your hands are trembling,
and your face is wrinkled
delicately.
The white hair on your cheek
quivers as you sleep,
Grandmother.

Lyn Lifshin

Family

virgin   she
must have been in that
sepia picture
lace to her teeth
marrying in the old house
a man she couldn't trust

lit candles 50 years
listened while he
pumped the hired
girl in the back den
how could she leave
with the four children
from him

moved to her
own sheets, watched
sun on glass elephants
thinking how it could
be with someone else,
getting old

at 70 she buries him,
finally she can't even hate
him and then the son she's
held closest

nothing moving in her
eyes now just husks that fall
apart if you touch them

the greenness gone someplace else

Carol Ascher

To My Grandmother
1876-1970

Suddenly you're gone and I see years ago
the snug apartment on Grand Boulevard
where with the ivory brush brought from Berlin
you sat combing your never-cut hair.
You had wide hair pins I'd never seen,
curling irons for side waves
and diamond pins you called broaches
and kept in a green velvet box
before you lost them and wore instead
the silver your son sent up from Mexico
where he now labored to cut perfect mirrors.

Did you once have fifty pairs of gloves
in every color? And did you wear them eating
as Mother said? Weeks ago
I saw in an old trunk, now in her basement
soiled kid, all lengths. Also veils, scarves.
You had been the Last Great Lady
and I was always pleased
trying on earrings or piling up my hair
to be shown the sepia photos proving
just how I looked like you.

You could be the Lady of Berlin
even while your sons and daughters
dug in the immigrant way.

Later in that tiny third-floor kitchen
your pale eyes grew pinlike defending
the scandalous pink dish set for twelve
you'd bought on your last solo shopping trip.
"Please, what guests are you expecting?"
demanded Mother, who went in search of a nursing home.
And I admired your disdain for the spotless dining hall
and your proud refusal to speak English
your clipped German baffling
the Jamaican attendants, who couldn't know
how grand you still were beneath the shrivelled skin.

Oh Queen of another country
dead, now dead
and a time is over.

Gail Kadison Golden

gifts

for Celia Posner

she sat amidst
the clutter of her life
my grandmother
and packed it
into shopping bags

two sets of dishes
one for meat
one for milk
pots, ladles
an iron cocker spaniel
that cracked nuts

into boxes, into bags
she prepared for
the second great migration
of her life
once from Russia
to the bowels of New York
now from Queens
to the beaches of Miami

leaving children
leaving children's children
looking for sun
and extra years of life

one pot she held back
here she said
you take this
it makes good soup
you remember?

I remembered
during the war
the army took my father
my mother took a job
my grandmother took me

frightened at first

piercing with effort
the thick Yiddish accent
I slipped into
the strange rhythm
of her days

fish markets we perused
(me with a father at war
frightened of so much deadness)
she stared the fish down
like so many cossacks
selecting only those
that dared to look back

we blitzed a dozen shops
a nickel here
a quarter there
accumulating feasts
from a pocket of change

my turn at last
she rested in the playground
play   she said
children should play

later she cooked
pots of soup
puddings and fish
sometimes when it
was my wish
I helped her
and she would share with me
the secrets of her craft
which seemed to me then
like *Kabbalah*

at other times
I did not wish to help
and then she would observe
later you'll have plenty
time to cook
so now you'll play
children should play

at night   the strange
peach colored apartment

filled with people
talking of war
on faded couches
waiting for telegrams
in musty halls

but each morning again
we were only two
marketing through a war
making a world
of playgrounds
and soup pots

when the war ended
my parents took me
half a continent away
from the peach
colored apartment

my grandmother cried
for weeks
I was silent
and did not smile

I never lived
with her again
we always kept in touch
by letter, by phone
by plane
in thoughts, in wishes
in dreams

we still keep in touch
I still have her pot

it always makes
wonderful soup

Janet Winans

On learning that the Russians have
occupied 2790 Green St.

Odd of them to put a consulate
where, all those years, grandparents lived.
Odd to see the building fortified
as if there were a way, a way to keep . . .
and odd imagining a clump of Russian bears
pressed fur to fur, the elevator
creeping up to 4, the double doors
you have to close just so . . .

I wonder if the Russians say hello
and disappear as we did, hurrying
to spread the Sunday comics on the bedroom floor;
if they know Grandma will look in
to ask why no one ever laughs . . .
On Green St. is the rice in little mounds,
a miniature igloo on each dinner plate?
Are red and green and yellow sourballs still there
all afternoon inside the cheek?

Strange, the roof a maze of radar now,
their listening devices in the walls, invisible . . .
I wonder if they strain against the paneling
and hear our mutterings in Hebrew,
sip our purple wine. I wonder
if they breathe the smoke that we did,
candles, Chesterfields, cigars.

Overnight their flag, their crest
above a door whose weight I still can feel . . .
Have they discovered how the black piano plays
with no one's fingers on the keys?
Do they know how to start the roll,
the lever right for fast or left for slow
but gently, paper tears so easily . . . it's not a toy . . .
there's no one anymore to fix these things.

Linda Watskin

Immigrant

My grandmother's hands
held crochet needles,
fashioned lace webs
of beige thread.

She baked honey cake
in pans,
bought from a peddler
whose tongue stumbled
over English.

She skinned potatoes
into slivers,
watched them dance
in an iron skillet.

Her hands
moved slow
enough to hold.
They held
my face
until they became
part of me.

I taught her to write
her name in American.
She taught me to rest
my head between her breasts
and listen.

Lyn Lifshin

I Was Four, In Dotted

Swiss summer pajamas
my face a blotch of
measles in the small
dark room over blue
grapes and rhubarb,
hot stucco cracking
17 North Seminary
that july Friday
noon my mother was
rushed in the grey
blimp of a Chevy
north to where my
sister Joy would be
born two months
early. I wasn't
ready either and
missed my mother's
cool hands, her
bringing me frosty
glasses of pineapple
juice and cherries
with a glass straw
as Nanny lost her
false teeth, flushed
them down the toilet
then held me so tight
I could smell lavender
and garlic in her
braided hair   held
me as so few ever
have since   as if
not to lose more

Sauci S. Churchill

Aunt Iris' Wedding

Except for just a moment
the wedding was a success
although the rabbi was late
and the little flower girl
could not be persuaded
to go down the aisle.
The old ones had their schnapps
and someone lost false teeth
in a potted plant.

Irresistible in pale pink tulle,
the flower girl was passed across the table,
passed among the uncles over spilled food
and blood red wine, dropping petals
on the hands that grabbed and
pinched in admiration.

She was spun like cotton candy
from Uncle Julius to Uncle Max.
Above the flames of a candelabra
her fairy dress caught like tinder
melting the diaphanous net,
until the hands of her *baubi* found her,
smothered the flames against her breast.

Toni Mergentime Levi

Fat

Sensing behind her back
that I had slimmed,
my grandmother turned
from her pot of stock,
frowned and warned,
"Skinny is no good."

She was afraid
death would move in
among her boarders,
who had no mates or teeth
to guard them as they slept.
And slowly he would skim
the fat off—
if you had enough to satisfy,
you might survive.

Grandma wore her fat
like a ruff below her chin
and a vest beneath her apron.
She worried hard to see me
slipping out the door at seventeen
dressed only in my nerves and bones.

Barbara Noreen Dinnerstein

Bubbie, Mommy, Weight Watchers and Me

The lady up in front was Rosalie, she used to be fat, *feh*. My mommy told me she was the lecture. I mean she showed us pictures of herself when she was fat. She told us to put a picture of ourselves on the 'fridgerator of us eating and looking really fat and ugly. She said remember what you look like. Remember how ugly you are. The picture Mommy picked out of me was one of me at *Bubbie's* house.

It was *Rosh Hashana*. We were eating honey cake that *Bubbie* and I made. We spent the whole afternoon in the kitchen cooking and baking for when company came for *Shabbos*. *Bubbie* told me if she wanted to have a sweet New Year she had to eat sweet things, so she kept nibbling on my fingers. We baked a round *hallah* to hide under the towel for when *Zayde* came home. Then we would all sit at the big table and *Zayde* would say the prayers. *Bubbie*, Mommy and me would do the candles. Then we would eat. I even got to sneak a sip of my mom's wine.

In the picture I was sitting between *Bubbie* and Mommy. I don't think I looked ugly there, just happy. Why did she have to pick that picture to scotch tape on the refrigerator? My brother Leonard who always made fun of me saw that picture on the refrigerator. He drew a lot of flies all around me. Why did mom have to pick a picture of me at a time when I felt so warm and safe and let Leonard draw flies all around me?

Even things at *Bubbie's* house changed. Mommy made *Bubbie* promise not to feed me anymore. No more egg creams, no more tea in a glass with a sugar cube between our teeth, no more *mandle brot* and no more *lokshen kugel* and no more honey cake. My *Bubbie* always told me I had the sweetest *tushy*. Rosalie called it your grotesque buttocks. My *tushy* didn't seem different to me, no matter what Rosalie called it.

Bubbie told me Rosalie used to be *mispochah* until she married "that *Shaygetz* Stanley." *Bubbie* told me Mommy was becoming too American. She said that Mommy was forgetting who her people were. I didn't understand, then. Mommy stopped calling me *knadle* and told *Bubbie* to speak English to me, no Yiddish. My *Bubbie* still called me her *shayneh maidel*, told me I had the best *tush* and still fed me. It became our secret.

Bubbie was proud, she'd say, "Never forget who you are, who your people are. You are from peasant stock, hardy, built to survive. We are not Americans, just like we were not Russians, we are travellers on a long road waiting to go home again. This diet stuff of your mother's is just another way to pretend we belong.

Jews don't belong. Be proud, be strong, be who you are. Someday we will have a home, someday we will be able to look like Jews and be proud."

Next to my *Bubbie*, my Mommy was my best friend. Just like *Bubbie* and me, Mommy and I used to cook together and play together in the kitchen. She would tell me stories about growing up on the Lower East Side and about her *Bubbie* Bayla. I would tell her all my secrets and she would promise me they were safe. My Mommy made me laugh at her singing *Sunrise Sunset* and the *Boogie Woogie Bugle Boy* for the millionth time. She would dance all over the kitchen singing into the ladle like it was a microphone. Sometimes we laughed so hard we wet our pants.

When my Mommy lost all that weight, we stopped singing and talking and playing in the kitchen. She apologized to me for making me sick. I didn't understand what she meant. I thought all those things we did together were the best. She said she made me sick like her and that is why I had to go to Weight Watchers. She told me I had to think of the future, getting boyfriends and stuff. I didn't know how to tell her I didn't want boyfriends and stuff. I liked what we did.

To this day I don't understand what she was talking about, those moments with her were precious. I yearn for that time I spent in the kitchen with my mom and my *Bubbie*, warm and safe, braiding the *hallah*, mushing the *knadles*, licking the spoons, telling the secrets, making eat for the family, laughing and crying.

When my *Bubbie* died, before I threw my handful of dirt on her coffin to say goodbye, I promised her I would never forget who I am and where my people come from. I am proud to look the way I do. I am a strong proud Jewish woman from peasant stock.

Myra Shapiro

The Corset

The corset of my *Bubbe* Annie
held her to the feminine
symmetry of her youth—an immigrant
sent South to help her uncle
tend his store (I want to shelter her—
the broken English, the strangeness
of a Jew, of her body
at fourteen)
She was alone.
Four boys ganged her.
For one year she had to stay inside
the safety of a place for the insane.

Home, North, the Coops on Bronx Park East,
she met her husband whose artistic,
fluent ways enabled her
to ripple like a fountain. She grew fat

so that each morning, bone by bone,
a corset laced the chaos to its parts:
full breasts, slim waist, round hips—
an eight to match my age
those summer nights I shared her room
and saw the miracle, how, stay by stay,
lace by lace, she loosened the reined flesh
and sent it tumbling—*ahh a machaiah!*—
fold by fold, sigh by sigh, the drench of it
so delicious I told everyone
when I was grown I wanted fat like hers
rushing over me as unrestrained as water.

Elaine Starkman

Sharing the Wisdom

for Malka Heifetz Tussman
(1896-1987)

You come, old one,
to my bones that ache from
frantic movements of midlife

My mind hangs on mortality
like the rain on this roof,
its hum your defiant heart

I see you in your
Berkeley flat, alone, unafraid
eyes weak, visions strong
knuckles bent on your blazing pen

Have you a contract with God?
What holy tongue did He whisper
in your ear? What wisdom did
He blow into your soul?

Tell me as I drag to dinner
wearing the memory of
your thin frame and silvered mind,
a talisman against growing old

Andrea Hollander Budy

Elegy

for Esther Goldberger Hollander

June,
and you are gone at ninety-one.
Old enough,
someone says as he nods away my grief.
But you are not all that died.
There are those stories of your youth
you never told, and the places, those people
I long to hold through your words.
Now there is no one left who speaks
those Yiddish dreams
born before either of us.
I remember your European braids and your face
with its history of Jewish pain,
and I want to know more than I know.
You son, my dad, looks back and sees little.
I see less.
What will my children see?
The moon swells each night with the same news,
or worse—it shrinks, that brief light,
that sabbath candle at no one's table. Grandma,
who will say the evening blessing?

Lesléa Newman

Legacy

I.
How They Came

Two came from Russia
and two from Hungary
arriving in New York
all four strangers.
Two of them met in a deli in Brooklyn
and two of them met in a place forever
        on their lips underground.
Each two met and married and bore three children
like the six tips of a Jewish star
        pointing towards eternity.
One of the three
met one of the three
in a high school in Brooklyn,
met and married and bore three children as well,
one of whom grew up
to arrive on this snowy morning of her 30th year
strong, beautiful and me.

II.

I look at my life:
these hands those feet
this face that belly,
all mine.
This table those chairs
these plants those pots
that rug this bed
somehow we have all arrived.

I look at my life:
some days are calm as a glass of water
        high on an empty shelf
some days are stormy as a raging ocean
        crashing against the rocks, bruising the shore
some days I have left behind
some days I have left

I look at my life:

it is nothing
but a miracle
these sheets those shoes
this head that hair
this heart
it is no accident
I am here

III.

Grandma, how old were you when you came here?
I don't remember.
Do you remember the boat ride? Do you remember
      Ellis Island?
What's there to remember? I'm an old lady,
      it's not so important. Eat some soup.
But Grandma, I want to know something about
      your life. Tell me a story.
Tell? What's there to tell? I'm an old lady.
Some days my feet hurt bad, some days my feet hurt
not so bad. You want some chicken? Here, take this piece,
it's not so dry. Listen, I'll tell you one thing.
The most important thing is your health. You have your health,
you have everything. And I'll tell you one more thing.
The worst thing is to be alone. Some days I talk to the walls
just to have someone to talk to. Some nights I'm afraid
to fall asleep, I should wake up dead and no one would know.
Believe me thirty years is a long time to be alone.
Maybe I should have married again, but who would think
I should live so long? You finished the chicken,
good *Mamala*, have some applesauce. You're such a good girl
shayneh maideleh, *oy* you should only get married
and live a long happy life.

IV.

Lesléa Newman
daughter of Florence Newman
daughter of Ruth Levin
daughter of Fannie Zuckerman
daughter of Minukha

Minukha
mother of Fanny Zuckerman
mother of Ruth Levin
mother of Florence Newman

mother of Lesléa Newman
mother of

Where I have come from is where I will go

Now I am the mother
of my own life
I have created it
I have nurtured it
I have held it in my hand
I have let it go

May my mother
and her mother
and her mother
and all the mothers before that
who have carried me in their wombs
a tiny secret, a treasure, a joy, a hope, a dream
may they all be proud of who I am
and what I have done

For I am the last daughter
and my life is a precious stone
a cut and carved and polished jewel
that will brighten the world
for an instant
like a pair of *Shabbos* candles
whose flames reflect
in a kitchen window
in a *Kiddish* cup
in somebody's dark eyes
before fading, flickering
and finally surrendering
to the night

Gail Kadison Golden

Morning

it is eight o'clock in
the morning and the phone
rings it is my mother
who is in Florida visiting her mother
and my mother is calling to say
that my grandmother is dying

and I do not know what to feel
because my grandmother is almost 95
she is sick she is in pain
has told me now for several months
that she is ready to die in fact
would like to die
so I would like to accept that this is her
wish but I do not want her to die
(in all of my life
when I have looked for her
I have known where to find her)

and I know that before the day is over
I will cry but I will not cry now
because I am serving breakfast and my
oldest needs help with her homework
but finally I can not
and I say "today I can not help you"
and her eyes look like green shattered glass

but I am on a swing
I am swinging high over the park
and my grandmother is watching me
when suddenly I fall off the swing
and my grandmother is holding my head
which is bleeding and she is crying
and I am crying
and she is crying harder than I am

for Thanksgiving dinner
we eat turkey we have gravy
there is also cranberry sauce
in the afternoon my aunt calls
to say that the doctors
want to give my grandmother

94

a pacemaker
but my grandmother said no
so the doctors explained things
very carefully and asked her again
and she said no

for months now
the phone calls between
my grandmother
and myself
are brief
there is little
that she wants
little left that she can give
only "you will remember grandma?"
and I say "Yes
I will remember"
I will remember that always
when I have looked for her
I have known where
to find her

December starts out warm
in Manhattan with friends
to see a concert
I do not even need a coat
(before the rich strong music
comes to an end
my grandmother will
draw a last sleeping breath
in a place far away
from where I am)

it is eight o'clock in the morning
when the phone rings it is my mother
calling to say that
my grandmother is dead

birds fly frightened past my window
through darkened skies
they are going south
to my grandmother
how will they find her

my grandmother's mother
lies in an unmarked grave somewhere

in Russia bones heaped upon
other bones the casual litter
of some casual *pogrom*

my grandmother's grave will be marked
for this
she was
triumphant

on the phone again my mother
is saying
I have cooked chicken
but now I will have to freeze it
she is saying laundry
I have to do laundry
I say MA
how do you feel
she says I don't
I don't feel
I say MA I love you
she says what what
I say I love you
and she cries

the last time I saw my grandmother
I held her dying frailness against me
and wondered
grandma in what dream
did you carry me
in what lost worlds
did you shield me with such force
that the terrors of a world at war
faded into the folds
of your ill-fitting dress

the last time I saw my grandmother
I went to kiss her goodbye
and she turned her back to me
clenching her teeth
go she said don't say anything
just go
and I did
taking with me as always
the ferocity of her love

mother of my mother

by your thin blue veined hands
I have been anointed
strong

upon learning of the death of my grandmother
a friend places one red rose
on my desk
I watch it grow from red
to crimson to black
and still I can not let it go

soon the petals will fall away
and when I look for my grandmother
where shall I go to find her

Louise Steinman

Last Earthwords for Awhile

Answer this question: if a train is moving at forty kilometers an hour, and a frightened child with Czarist rubles sewn into the pocket of her dress jumps off into a field of beets, how old will she be when she returns home?

The story passes to me secondhand, from my brother Larry, the doctor. Grandma is already dead a week, though Larry assured me she'd pull through. "After all," he'd said, "can someone be about to die if they're still telling new stories?"

My father-in-law sent me, with Schlomo and Itzhak to Kiev. To exchange Czarist rubles for gold. Into my dress I sewed a pouch, and I closed it with—what do you call them—diaper pins? If you see soldiers, throw the money off the train, my father told me.

We are on the train going home to Zhitomir. So crowded on the train. Then, we hear soldiers. They search everybody, moving from car to car. We don't wait. We run into a car they look in already and hide behind a sack of wheat. Quietly, our hearts pounding, we climb to the roof of one of the cars. Itzhak pulls my hand. We jump.

We walk back to Zhitomir. Everybody there stands around, crying and crying. They scream, so happy to see us. Why you crying? we ask. Soldiers, they say, they murder everybody on the train, everybody in the station.

A rainy Los Angeles morning for her burial. The Hollywood sign is visible on the hill through the fog. My nephew and I are the only ones who peer into the open casket. She prepared for this moment, her best blue dress pressed and ready for years. The note she had written in her childlike hand, how she didn't want flowers. She is smiling.

I dream of her. I am in a beetfield in the Ukraine. A farmer is harvesting. His tractor raises clouds of dust in a loud mechanical chatter. Through the dust, at the far end of the field, I see a figure in long skirts sitting on the ground. As I walk towards her, my feet mark the moist soil. I sit down beside my grandmother. She takes my face tenderly in both her hands.

"Listen," she says, "everything is unbelievable, but what can we do?"

Yiddish and Hebrew Glossary*

Babooshka - scarf tied around the head
Bissl - a little
Brocha - blessing
Bubbe (also **Baubi, Bobba, Bubbie**) - Grandmother
Challah - braided bread used on *Shabbos* and other festivals
Chanukah (H) - Festival of lights, lasting eight days and commemorating the Maccabees' victory over the Syrians and the rededication of the Temple at Jerusalem
Der gantser velt - the whole world
Derma - intestines; stuffed *derma* is a delicacy
Du - you
Du gedenkst - you remember
Du kenst nit hobn - you cannot have
Feh - ugh
Fingerl - ring
Fooseleh - little foot
Gefilte fish - chopped fish cakes
Hanteleh - little hand
Huppa - wedding canopy
Ikh - I
Ikh gedenk nit - I don't remember
Ikh vil - I want
Kabbalah (H) - Jewish mysticism
Keppeleh - head
Kiddish (H) - blessing
Klayn - little
Knadles - *matzo* balls
Kosher - fit to eat, according to Jewish dietary law
Kreplach - dumpling
Kugel - pudding made from noodles, potatoes or *matzo*
Kvell - take pleasure in
Loschen - language
Machaiah - great pleasure
Maideleh (also **maidel, maydelech**) - girl
Mame - mother
Mame loschen - mother tongue, Yiddish
Mameleh- (also **mamala, mamela**) endearment, literally "little mother"
Mandlebreit (also **mandle brot**) - almond cake
Mandlin - almonds
Matzo - unleavened bread
Matzo brei - *matzo* mixed with eggs and fried in butter
Mazel tov - good luck, congratulations
Meisehs - stories

---

*(H) designates all words in Hebrew

Mezuzeh (also **mezzuzah**) - small container affixed to the right doorjamb of a Jewish home, containing verses from Deuteronomy

Minyan (H) - The quorum of ten people [traditionally men] required to be present for a religious service.

Mispochah - family

Mit- with

Naches - proud pleasure

Nayn - no

Oma (German) - grandmother

Opa (German) - grandfather

Oy - expression of fear, surprise, joy, pain, exhaustion, contentment etc.

Pesach - eight day celebration of the Jews' liberation from slavery and their Exodus from Egypt

Pogrom - an organized massacre of Jews

Punam (also **punim**) - face

Rosh Hashana - Jewish New Year

Rozhinkes - raisins

Rugelach - pastries, often filled with sugar and cinnamon

Seder (H) - traditional meal eaten first two nights of *Pesach*

Shabbos (also **Shabbat**) **(H)** - Sabbath

Shaygetz - a non-Jewish man (non-complimentary)

Shayneh (also **shana**) - beautiful

Sheytl - wig

Shiva - seven day mourning period

Shtetl- Jewish village

Shul - synagogue

Shvester - sister

Talmud (H) - body of literature interpreting the *Torah*

Tefillin (H) - phylacteries containing Biblical quotations which are strapped to the head and arms of Jewish men during morning prayers

The Forward - American Yiddish newspaper

Torah (H) - first five books of the Old Testament

Tsouris - troubles

Tush - buttocks

Velt - world

Yom Kippur - Day of Atonement

Zaydie (also **Zede**) - grandfather

Contributors' Notes

CAROL ASCHER'S most recent book is *The Flood*, a novel. She is the author of *Simone De Beauvoir: A Life of Freedom*. Her stories have appeared widely, and she is the recipient of three PEN/NEA Syndicated Short Fiction awards. She was born in 1941 in Cleveland, Ohio.

NANCY BERG was born in White Plains, New York, October 26, 1955. Her poetry has been published in over 45 magazines, journals and anthologies. She earned her M.A. in screenwriting from Stanford University. Nancy is a great lover of Broadway musicals and therein lie her dreams.

ANDREA HOLLANDER BUDY was born 28 April 1947 in Berlin, Germany. She now lives in Mountain View, Arkansas. Her two chapbooks are *Living on the Cusp* (Moonsquilt Press, 1981), and *Happily Ever After* (Panhandler Press, 1989), winner of the 1988 Panhandler Press Chapbook Series.

SAUCI S. CHURCHILL (nee Schwartz, b. 1940 Chicago) attended Wisconsin and Berkeley, taught English and Art, works as law librarian to U.S. Nuclear Regulatory Commission, is currently with a Commission writing a report on high-level waste storage to be submitted to Congress in November.

ANNE COREY was born in Beth Israel Hospital, Manhattan, on November 2, 1947. She lives in Park Slope, Brooklyn. Her work has appeared in *Sinister Wisdom*, *We're Working On It*, and *Love Bytes*. She writes plays as well as poetry and fiction.

MARYLYN CROMAN was born in Brooklyn in 1936. She has been a freelance writer and editor for the past 18 years. She teaches free lance article writing in San Antonio, Texas, and in the past few years has started writing poetry.

BARBARA NOREEN DINNERSTEIN is a cute, funny Jewish butch who happens to be fat, deaf, and in recovery. Born in Newark, New Jersey in 1958, she lives in San Francisco and is "differently pleasured."

JOAN (THALER) DOBBIE: I was born on January 12, 1946 in Switzerland; my family escaped from Vienna. I grew up in a small Northern New York town, my grandparents just up the street. I have an M.F.A. in Creative Writing from the University of Oregon. I write poems, teach poetry, do art work, practice and teach Hatha Yoga. I have two children, Dawn (19) and Andy (14).

SUSAN EISENBERG was born in 1950 in Cleveland, Ohio and grew up in a 3-generation household with her sister, parents, grandmother, and a cat to keep the peace. Transplanted to Boston, she alternates as a poet/writer and electrician.

DIANE GARDEN: I was born in St. Louis, Missouri on January 6, 1946. I am a professor at Michigan State University. I have published poems in *The Jewish Spectator, Présence Africaine,* and *MidAmerica,* and I won the 1988 Gwendolyn Brooks Poetry award.

SANDRA GARDNER: Born 5/22/40 in Massachusetts. Her poetry—often mythic, sometimes feminist, and nearly always ironic—has appeared in a number of publications. She is working on a second edition of her third non-fiction book and the beginnings of her fourth.

GAIL KADISON GOLDEN, Ed.D. was born 7/11/43 in Florida. She is a psychotherapist and poet living in New York with her husband and two daughters. She is grateful for this book since she promised Celia Posner, her grandmother, that she would be remembered.

LISA GOODMAN was born in New York City thirty one years ago, and continues to reside there. She has recently completed a novella based upon her experiences in the Soviet Union.

PAMELA GRAY, born 1956 in Brooklyn, is a poet and playwright living in Oakland. Her work appears in *New Lesbian Writing* and *Politics of the Heart.* Her Meema would have bought at least ten copies of this book.

JUDYTH HILL was born February 13, 1953 in New Jersey. She is the owner of the Chocolate Maven Bakery in Santa Fe, New Mexico. She also teaches writing classes for adults and children.

MARGO HITTLEMAN was born on May 28, 1959 in Queens, New York and now makes her home in Ithaca, New York. She is fascinated by family histories and hopes someday to further explore the institutionalization of immigrant women.

RUTH HARRIET JACOBS, Ph.D., born November 15, 1924 in Boston, earned a Brandeis Ph.D. at 45, has authored five books, taught at universities and is a scholar at the Wellesley College Center for Research on Women.

IRENE JAVORS, born Brooklyn, New York, August 31, 1948, psychotherapist, poet, author of poetry volume, *Mists of Memory* (Empress, Wales, U.K. 1988).

MARILYN KALLET (12/28/46) was born in Montgomery, Alabama. Her poems have appeared in *New Letters, Greensboro Review* and *Denver Quarterly.* She won the 1988 Tennessee Arts Commission Literary Fellowship in Poetry, and is Director of Creative Writing at the University of Tennessee, Knoxville.

SUSAN KAN makes her home in Northampton, Massachusetts. "The Lost Pearl" is her first published poem. She was born September 28, 1962 in Chevy Chase, Maryland.

JESSE KULBERG: I was born in New York (Brooklyn). Have worked in movies—particularly at Twentieth Century Fox. Have published plays, articles, and short stories. My age? Never mind.

TONI MERGENTIME LEVI, poet and librettist (born 7/29/41, NYC), has published poems in numerous journals, including, *Crosscurrents*, *Kansas Quarterly* and *Texas Review*. She and her husband, composer Paul Alan Levi, are now writing their second opera.

SUSAN (RITTER) LEVINKIND: I'm 47, an Ashkenazi lesbian, mother, librarian, teacher, writer. When I moved from Massachusetts to California, my *Bubbe*, who left Russia to find freedom in America, visited my dreams to give me courage.

LYN LIFSHIN (born 1949, Burlington, Vermont) has published more than eighty poetry books and chapbooks. She has edited a series of women's writing: *Tangled Vines* (Beacon Press); *Ariadne's Thread* (Harper and Row); and *Lips Unsealed* (forthcoming from Capra Press).

ROCHELLE SHAPIRO NATT: I was born November 23, 1947 in Rockaway Beach, New York. Although I've published in many anthologies and won awards from various places, my real purpose is to leave a legacy of my past to my children, Charles and Heather.

KAREN NEUBERG: I was born 5/10/44 in Brooklyn, New York. My poems have been published in *The Little Magazine*, *Scrivener*, and *Touchstone*. I have been associated with a writing group, Poet's Union, for ten years. "In Your Dough Kitchen" was awarded a first prize in poetry at the 1987 Philadelphia Writers Conference.

LESLÉA NEWMAN'S biographical information appears at the end of the book.

IRENE RETI: I was born April 27, 1961 in Los Angeles, California. I am happy when I have time to write in the midst of running HerBooks and editing Oral History publications at UC Santa Cruz. I am the daughter of two refugees from the Holocaust, and found out I was Jewish at age 17.

CASSANDRA SAGAN was born in Brooklyn October 1, 1954. She now lives on the San Juan Ridge in the Sierra foothills, where she is a poet, teacher and mother of 2.

LYNN SAUL: Born Long Beach, California, 1945, grew up in Pittsburgh, have lived in and near Tucson since 1971. I now live on the Tohono O'Odham Indian Reservation, where I teach writing for Pima College and work as a legal services attorney.

DEBORAH ESTHER SCHIFTER, born 1951, Washington, D.C., lives in Amherst, Massachusetts with her husband and works in mathematics education. She is currently translating the correspondence between her grandparents, Paul and Balbina Schifter, and her father.

KAREN SEXTON-STEIN was born in Brooklyn, New York in 1960. Her work has appeared in many anthologies and magazines, including *World Treasury of Great Poems*, *Mysteries of the Lyric World*, *It's On My Wall*, *Free Focus*, *Pegasus*, *People Watcher*, and *Peace Newsletter*.

MYRA SHAPIRO, born in the Bronx in 1932, recently returned to New York after 45 years in Georgia and Tennessee. She received the Dylan Thomas Poetry Award from The New School and two MacDowell Colony fellowships.

SUSAN SHAPIRO was born January 23, 1961. She moved from Michigan to Manhattan eight years ago. Her writing has appeared in *The New York Times Book Review, New York Newsday, New York Woman, Folio, Glamour, Present Tense, Lilith* and other publications.

LINDA SHEAR Born 1948, Chicago, I am a Jewish lesbian singer, songwriter and C.P.A. living in the foothills of the Berkshire mountains of Massachusetts with my partner/lover Windflower and our two dogs, Tana and Sandy.

MARCY SHEINER was born the first day of Spring in the first year following World War II (March 21, 1946) in Manhattan. Her work has appeared in *Mother Jones* magazine and many poetry journals. She is currently living in San Francisco, where she is writing a novel.

ENID SHOMER: Born February 2, 1944 in Washington, D.C. Her *Stalking the Florida Panther* won The Word Works' book prize. Her poems and stories appear in *Poetry, Ploughshares, Tikkun, Midstream,* etc. In 1989 she received a fellowship from the National Endowment for the Arts.

JOAN SELIGER SIDNEY: I was born on 19 September 1942 in Jersey City, New Jersey, the daughter of refugees from the Holocaust. Four children, a doctorate, and several jobs later, I began to write, leading to my recent MFA.

CYNTHIA SOBSEY: Born 12/13/20 and raised in New York City. Published in *Passages North* and *Swamproot.* Winner of Andrew Mountain Poetry contest "Voices International." Completing poetry chapbook entitled "US."

BETH A. SPIEGEL (born 1957, Los Angeles, California) lives with her husband Martin who tells bad jokes, and a cat named Monster in Pasadena, California, where she paints, works on picture book ideas, and edits documentary films for television.

SUSAN FANTL SPIVACK: I am a Storyteller performing traditional, contemporary, family and my own stories. I teach writing workshops in public schools. My work has appeared in *Blueline, Groundswell, Kalliope, Images, Mildred* and the *National Storytelling Journal.*

ELAINE MARCUS STARKMAN was born in Chicago in 1937. Presently she lives in California. She is co-editing the anthology, *Without a Single Answer: Poems of Contemporary Israel,* to be published by the Judah Magnus Museum of Berkeley, California, Spring 1990.

JUDITH STEINBERGH (born 1943, Kentucky) has published three books of poetry, her most recent being *A Living Anytime* (Troubadour Press). She co-authored, along with Elizabeth McKim, *Beyond Words, Writing Poems With Children*. She is currently writer-in-residence in the Brookline, Massachusetts public schools.

LOUISE STEINMAN is the author of *The Knowing Body: Elements of Contemporary Performance and Dance* (Shambhala Publications, 1986). She was born in Los Angeles in 1951, and, much to her amazement, lives there again today.

BARBARA UNGER was born in Woodside, Queens on October 2, 1932. She is a Professor of English at Rockland Community College of The State University of New York. Four books of her poetry have appeared. A short fiction collection is due in 1990.

LINDA WATSKIN: I was born in the Bronx, New York, live and teach in Massachusetts and love traveling to the Southwest with Dorothy. My poems have appeared in *Backbone*, *Rhino*, *Oyez Review*, and elsewhere.

CAROLYN WHITE: Born in 1948 in Brooklyn, resident of Michigan, I have traveled throughout Europe and am now living in Paris, France. I am a folklorist and storyteller. My first novel, *Ghostroad* (Creative Arts Book Co. of Berkeley) comes out in October, 1989.

ANNE WHITEHOUSE, poet, fiction writer, and freelance critic, was born 1/30/54 in Birmingham, Alabama. She is the author of *The Surveyor's Hand* (poems, published under Anne Cherner), and recently completed a first novel, *Resonance*.

JANET WINANS, born 5/10/33, San Francisco. B.A., Antioch College, Yellow Springs, Ohio. Married, three children. Careers: teacher, camp director, bookseller, librarian, poet. 1987, MFA, Poetry; Warren Wilson College, Swannanoa, N.C. Currently Artist-in-Education, Arizona Arts Commission.

GENE ZEIGER is a poet and fiction writer whose work has appeared in many journals including *The New York Times Book Review* and *The Georgia Review*. Her collection of poems, *Sudden Dancing*, was recently published. She was born in 1943, in New York City.

DEBORAH ZUCKER was born in Milwaukee, Wisconsin on July 21, 1956. She works as a family therapist and organization consultant in Philadelphia, PA.

Editor Lesléa Newman, age 33, with her grandmother Ruth Levin, age 99.

About the Editor

Lesléa Newman has written and published a novel, two poetry collections, a short story book, a children's book and a play. Her work has appeared in many magazines and anthologies and in 1989 she was awarded a Massachusetts Artists Fellowship in Poetry. All of her work is very strongly influenced by her identity as a Jew and as a lesbian. "I write/edit the kind of books I want to read," she says. Lesléa makes her living by teaching women's writing workshops and lecturing at colleges and various other institutions. And, just in case you're wondering, her grandmother is very, very proud.

Also By Lesléa Newman

Fiction
Good Enough To Eat
A Letter To Harvey Milk

Poetry
Just Looking For My Shoes
Love Me Like You Mean It

Children's Books
Heather Has Two Mommies

Plays
After All We've Been Through

Cover Photo: Editor Lesléa Newman and her grandmother, Ruth Levin, Brighton Beach, 1956.